# Praise for *Pi*

In *Primed To Lead*, Chris has brought us a practical and readable book that gives the inner workings of leadership. Each chapter has great insights with contemporary illustrations, along with reflection points and coaching moments. As Chris says so well: "If you and I can't be led ourselves, then we have no business leading other people." This is a terrific book to hone your skills or to teach leadership principles to another person.

**Dr. David Fletcher,**
Founder of XPastor—Expanding the
Business Brain + Pastoral Heart

I wish I had had a resource like *Primed to Lead* when I began in ministry almost 40 years ago. Chris' insight both from his own practical experience as a church leader and other leaders he leans into for wisdom make this a great place to start for any new leader.

**Geoff Surratt,** Multisite Strategist @
MinistryTogether.com

I am fortunate to call Chris Warszawski a personal friend and have admired his leadership for years. In *Primed to Lead*, he shares invaluable wisdom and practical learning that will challenge you and catalyze your leadership growth. *Primed to Lead* is a book you will want to make a part of your foundational leadership library.

**Sherry Surratt,** Executive Director of
Leadership Strategy, Orange

*Primed To Lead* is a must-read for anyone aspiring to become an effective leader. This book is filled with clear, compelling principles that will encourage and equip you to lead like Jesus in any leadership context.

**Dan Owolabi,** Author of *Authentic Leadership*

If we want to reach the next generation for Christ then we need to be investing in the next generation of leaders. *Primed To Lead* provides coaches and mentors the opportunity to do just that!

**Kary Oberbrunner,** Author of *Your Secret Name, Elixir Project, Unhackable*

*Primed to Lead* is an excellent resource for emerging leaders and anyone who's coaching or mentoring emerging leaders. Whether you are new to leadership or stepping into a new leadership role, Chris' book provides practical action steps to consider as you embrace the challenge to lead.

**Troy Palermo,** Executive Pastor, Lifepoint Church

# PRIMED TO LEAD

## AN HONEST CONVERSATION
## FOR NEW & EXPERIENCED LEADERS

### CHRIS WARSZAWSKI

Printed in the United States of America

Published by Author Academy Elite
PO Box 43, Powell, OH 43065
www.AuthorAcademyElite.com

Identifiers:
Library of Congress Control Number: 2020910924
ISBN: 978-1-64746-333-5 (paperback)
ISBN: 978-1-64746-334-2 (hardback)
ISBN: 978-1-64746-335-9 (ebook)

Available in paperback, hardback, e-book, and audiobook

Scripture quotations are from the ESV® Bible (The Holy Bible, English
Standard Version®), copyright © 2001 by Crossway, a publishing
ministry of Good News Publishers. Used by permission.
All rights reserved.

Any Internet addresses (websites, blogs, etc.) printed in this book are
offered as a resource. They are not intended in any way to be or imply an
endorsement by Author Academy Elite, nor does Author Academy Elite
vouch for the content of these sites and numbers for the life of this book.

Some names and identifying details have been changed to protect the
privacy of individuals.

*To my best team –*
*My loving and supportive wife, Katie,*
*and my joy-giving kids, Ella and Jacob*

# CONTENTS

## CULTIVATING INFLUENCE

## CREATING MOVEMENT

# FOREWORD

There aren't that many *new* problems. However, we always have a new crop of leaders facing the same *old* problems in their generation.

About 80 years ago, Flora Klein had a problem.

At the young age of 14, she showed promise as a make-up artist. An older, middle-aged, influential woman recognized Flora's talent. For some time, Flora did the lady's make-up on a daily basis, making the older woman feel unique and special...covering her minor flaws...drawing attention to just the right spots. Daily, after having been made up, the lady would say and ask young Flora...

"Very good, Flora. *What's next?*"

Here was the problem—Flora was actually a prisoner of the Third Reich.

And the lady? She was the wife of the Commandant of the concentration camp that held Flora, her mother, and her aunt. Sadly, Flora's family members eventually fell prey to Hitler's extermination orders. However, the Commandant's wife would not allow Flora to meet the same fate.

*What happened next?*

After the war, Flora came to America and married. Eventually, she had a son, an artist named Eugene. He shared Flora's gifts of make-up and music, but he also possessed some of the flaws that can come with artistic gifts. Still, Eugene showed a unique work ethic that matched his artistic abilities. With each success in his early years, Flora would both encourage and ask her son:

"Very good, Eugene. *What's next?*"

In his later twenties, even when Eugene showed his mom a ten million-dollar check from the sale of his small make-up company, she again asked the very same question of what was next.

Eventually, Flora did stop asking Eugene *what was next* as her son became internationally renowned for bringing his unique brand of music and make-up together.

Who was this unique artist?

When Flora came to the US and married, she became Flora Simmons. And her son, Eugene Simmons, brought his unique brand of artistry in music and make-up to the band KISS.

Eugene's story began with a very simple question: *"What's next?"*

Just as every generation has its problems, in EVERY generation, we also ask questions. Hopefully, we aren't the victims of what C.S. Lewis called "chronological snobbery." We are NOT inherently smarter than our ancestors. We should look at the generation that *was* and comment, "Very good," and we should look at the generation that *is* and ask, "What's next?"

This is why *Primed To Lead* is so valuable for the next generation of leaders. It helps us to understand what is next for us as we step into leadership where we are, while also holding onto the very good that is behind us.

Chris Warszawski is a co-worker and a friend. He has the moral authority to write a book about leadership. While he is not perfect, he is humble and consistent in the leadership of his personal life, his family life, and his professional life. I'm grateful to be part of Chris' life and this work.

Dean Fulks
Lead Pastor, Lifepoint Church

# INTRODUCTION

I t was my time. Finally, I was being handed the keys. (Well, I guess there weren't literal keys involved, but you get what I'm saying.) It was a hot summer day when my Dad approached me and said, "How about *you* mow the lawn today?"

*Mow the lawn? All by myself?* For me, this was a serious rite of passage. I don't quite remember how old I was. Elementary-aged, for sure—but to me, age no longer mattered. I may have once been a boy, but now I was a man. And that man was going to mow the lawn all by himself. In fact, I was going to mow the lawn so well that it would look like the grounds crew for a professional athletic field had come and mowed. That mower and I were going to accomplish lawn greatness together. Or so I thought.

I made my way over to our garage and swiveled out the mower from the corner where it was neatly tucked. I grabbed our can of gasoline, unscrewed the tank cap on the engine, and filled it ever-so-neatly to the top. I even made sure the oil was full. Now, it was time to start that engine. I set my feet, grabbed the starter cord, and pulled back as fast and as hard as I could. And...*nothing*.

I knew that sometimes it took a couple of pulls to get the engine started, so I settled myself, grabbed the cord, and, with a grunt, yanked that cord back so hard it would have no choice but to start. Yet there wasn't even the slightest rumble from the engine.

Just to be sure, I checked the gas again. Full tank. I checked the oil again. It was full too. I examined the angle I was pulling from. Maybe I wasn't pulling back the correct way? I madly began pulling every which way I could. For the next half hour I exasperated myself pulling on that cord.

*Pull. Pull. PULL!* All I could do was pull. Yet, I went nowhere and accomplished nothing. I felt defeated, as though all my effort and energy spent had been for no good reason at all.

My father made his way back over and asked, "Chris, did you *prime* the engine?" I thought to myself, "*Prime the engine? What does that even mean?*"

My dad walked right over to the mower, stooped down to the corner of the engine, and found a little red button. "Here you go," he said as he used his thumb to press the button nine or ten times. "Go ahead; give it a pull now."

I was exhausted, but I mustered the strength for one last try. I grabbed the handle to the cord, set my feet, bent my knees, and ripped that handle back as if my life depended on it. A billowing cloud of smoke accompanied the beautiful roar of the engine. My heart leapt as I felt the mower handle shake in my hands. Finally, I was going to do what I had set out to do. That mower and I were ready to accomplish yard greatness together. All it took was a little priming.

## Trying To Lead

You may be wondering why I'm beginning a book on leadership with a story about a lawn mower. In a lot of ways this story illustrates my experience in the beginning days of trying to be a leader. I say *trying* because, while I might have stepped into different leadership roles, I wasn't really leading anyone anywhere. In fact, much like my younger self was pulling and pulling that lawn mower's starter cord to no avail, in those beginning days of leadership I found myself exasperated while accomplishing very little as a new leader.

Why is that? Because I wasn't *primed* to lead. Don't get me wrong—the resources were there. Just like I had the gas, the oil, and the mower capable of cutting that lawn, I had plenty of resources including wise mentors, a unique giftedness, and in my case a good education. Yet, there was still something I lacked. In the same way that I had overlooked the little red button on the mower, there were some simple, yet necessary, things missing in my heart and head that kept me from moving in the right direction (and from bringing others with me).

At the time of this writing, I've been serving in different leadership roles in churches for over a decade. Today, I am honored to be a leader of leaders who gets to encourage and coach others to have impact, and I love it. While I know that in no way have I arrived as a leader, I have learned how to begin well. However, that wasn't always the case. Honestly, when I first started in leadership I struggled mightily.

## An Espresso Mug Leader

Listen, I don't like stereotypes. I feel as though they put up unfair barriers and create unwarranted assumptions. Unfortunately, my lack of wisdom as a new leader took the liberty of building leadership barriers for me on its own.

Leadership guru John Maxwell talks about how we each have leadership capacity.[1] At certain points in my early days of leadership, my lack of wisdom probably led others to assume I had the leadership capacity of an espresso mug. (Don't get me wrong; I like espresso, but honestly those things are way too small.)

Others may have a similar story. For those who are considered either young or new in leadership, there are a lot of assumptions made, especially today. Many of us have heard the tired narrative about *millennials* (also known as Generation Y). Frankly, I don't think we need another book, podcast, or blog post on millennials (although some of them are actually very helpful). That's not the point of this book. The point of this book is to give new leaders what I didn't have when I started out in leadership and what I know a lot of current, impactful leaders wish they would've known when they began in leadership. In fact, throughout this book you're going to hear honest perspectives, real stories, and practical wisdom from experienced Christian leaders from all around the United States.

## Primed To Lead

In essence, my goal is to *prime* you with the biblical principles, practical habits, and effective strategies that will help you be a better leader, sooner. Whether you...

- Just began your first pastoral or ministry staff role at a church.

- Manage volunteers for a non-profit organization.

- Are in middle-management at a retail company.

- Lead a small group at your church.

- Recently made a career pivot.

- Or you just need fresh encouragement or a restart in your leadership.

So, wherever God has you or whatever leadership role He's placed you in, understand that **leadership** is meeting people where they are, cultivating the right to point them where they should go, and helping them to get there. *Primed to Lead* is designed to teach you just that as we focus on three key leadership competencies:

## 1. Starting Well

Starting (or re-starting) well in leadership requires having a secure anchor. It also requires us to have a clear vision for the legacy of our leadership. We'll learn how to investigate the culture of the organization we are a part of. This will equip us to better understand the people we serve, work with, and lead. We'll also cover why coaching, character, and excellence are paramount for every leader.

## 2. Cultivating Influence

Are you trustworthy? Our ability to cultivate influence begins with this question. Leaders who want to cultivate healthy influence will be servant leaders. We'll prioritize habits of presence and relational investment with the people we "rub shoulders" with consistently and discuss how to respond when we are invited into someone's pain. We'll cover why preparation makes all that we do better. And we'll look to the example of the most influential leader to ever walk the earth – Jesus Christ.

## 3. Creating Movement

As leaders we carry the role of *steward*, as well as *culture creator*. We'll talk about how to do both well. In order for our team to move where we actually want to go, we'll need to define our targets. We also need to create maps and parameters for how our team will work together to reach those targets. We'll cover other practical habits and effective strategies for leading teams.

## How To Use This Book

As you read through *Primed To Lead*, I've provided **Reflection & Discussion Questions** at the end of every chapter. These are meant for personal reflection and application of the principles, habits, and strategies of this book. If you're reading through the book with a small group, they are intended to catalyze discussion in your group time together.

*Primed To Lead* is especially designed for the context of coaching and mentorship. The chapters will help new and experienced leaders ("coaches") come alongside each other to have honest conversations around the material. The mentee and coach should read through the material individually and then define times to meet and utilize the **Coaching Moment** (at the end of each chapter) for discussion and practical application of the material.

If you are a new leader and don't have a coach that you are having conversations with as you read *Primed To Lead*, I would encourage you to consider finding one. To help you understand more of what a coach is, why having honest conversations with one is valuable, as well as how to find a coach, feel free to skip ahead to Chapter 2 to learn about coaches. Afterwards, you can return to Chapter 1.

## The Start Wasn't The End

Here's the happy middle of my story as a leader: my espresso mug-sized leadership capacity didn't stay small forever. God started adding clay. All of the sudden I was a bit more pliable and moldable, and He began to shape me as a leader. He used His Word to both widen and deepen my capacity. He brought in some other artists whose wisdom began to leave an imprint on my leadership. He even added heat to where I needed solidity.

My prayer is that God uses *Primed to Lead* to add a little clay, width, depth, artistry, and solidity to your leadership.

# STARTING WELL

# 1

# THE ANCHOR

Have you ever attempted to scale a climbing wall? I remember the first time I ever saw one. The monstrous gray wall had a face full of different shaped grips and offered three different paths that led to the ultimate goal: to ring the bell at the very top. Almost always, the ringing of the bell was accompanied by cheers from your peers who were spectating from down below.

This particular climbing wall was located at the summer camp I'd attended for years until high school graduation. After my freshman year of college, there was only one summer job I wanted, and it was to work at that summer camp.

Our camp staff team was comprised of mostly college students, and our job was to run all of the exciting activities of the camp. It was probably one of the most fun (and low-paying) jobs that a group of college students could have. At the beginning of summer, we all arrived for training, and each day we learned the ins and outs of how to care for the stable horses, lead trail rides, lifeguard the pond with its inflatables and slide, and run the ropes courses, including the climbing wall.

During our training, I learned something that had never occurred to me during all those years as a camp attendee. The most important role in climbing wasn't actually the climber. It was the belayer.

When it comes to climber safety, there is a system that involves not only wearing a helmet, harness, ropes, and hardware. Clutching the other end of a climber's rope is that important partner—the belayer. If a climber wants to scale the wall, he or she needs a secure belayer who knows the task at hand and can be trusted completely. Here's why:

- The belayer is the climber's **anchor**, keeping the climber in the air. Even if a climber slips off the wall, he or she won't crash to the ground because the belayer is anchoring the climber.

- The belayer **keeps a climber from injury** by pulling the climber's slack (extra rope). The extra slack can cause injury if the climber was to get tangled in the rope or fall.

- Finally, if the climber is tired and weary, the belayer can **provide rest** by lowering him or her down to safety.

## Who's Holding My Rope?

Leadership is a lot like scaling a climbing wall. Leaders have to define their goal, select the best path, take a lot of individual steps, and avoid gaps in order to accomplish the task. But the one question that not enough leaders, especially new leaders, ask is: *Who's holding the other end of my rope?*

The truth of the matter is too many of us enter leadership roles excited about the climb but without much thought as to what, or who, is keeping us secure and grounded. It's why so many leaders find themselves injured when they slip up, get tangled up, or need to let up and rest for a bit.

It's also a reason why many of us are apt to become weary or embittered. Then there are others who become stuck, feeling unable to move forward. Some of us struggle to slow down and let go of control of some things. What's the source of these leadership struggles? In our hearts, we're really not sure or confident about what or who is going to hold us up.

I have felt this as a leader. Early on in leadership I found myself quickly exhausted, frustrated and bitter. Bad habits began forming in my life. Selfishness and wanting to get my own way began to mire me down. A desire for control began to bubble to the surface. At the root of these bad habits was a faulty anchor in my life. I had placed my security as a leader in my own abilities. In other words, I had become my own anchor, and I've seen trusting this faulty anchor rear its ugly head in other leaders' lives as well. Why do we do this?

*Because a faulty anchor is always tethered to an inward fear.*

The reason we attach our security as leaders to faulty anchors, such as our own abilities, competency, and even relationships, is because we want some sense of control. And this need for control comes from fears deep within us.

These fears come in all different shapes and sizes. For some, we're just downright afraid of failure and what it might say about us. For others, we far too often hear the voices of people who made a profoundly discouraging impact on our lives, whether they did so with their words or actions. For some, we fear what those we respect may think of us.

Fear also exists in the climbing world. Climbers who have a belayer who they don't trust will always be insecure and handicapped by some kind of fear. But a climber who has a belayer who is completely trusted will always climb in freedom, even when the climber slips (and every climber slips). The truth of the matter is that if you and I are going to be healthy, effective leaders then we need something or someone who is going to keep us anchored, free, and rested.

• • •

We live in a culture that loves to prop up stories of self-sufficient, successful, "self-made" men and women. However, I have some news for you. None of us are "self-made." We all have a maker. In the Bible, Colossians 1 tells us that He was there at creation, and that all things, including you and me, were made by Him, through Him, and for Him. At this very moment He holds all of creation together. You and I, because of our evil deeds, were at odds with God. So, He offered a solution through His blood on a cross, and, as result, we could have peace with God again.

> *My hope is that you have responded to this Gospel (or "good news") by trusting in Jesus Christ for salvation. This means placing your faith in Him and the truth that His life, death, and resurrection are perfectly enough to grant you the forgiveness, status, and peace with God that you need.*[1]

> *Having a vibrant, personal relationship with God through Jesus Christ is everything – and my hope is that you have experienced this relationship. If you have not, or if you find yourself discouraged in some way, I encourage you to take steps toward Him: have a conversation with a friend who you know is a Christian, get connected to a Bible-believing church, and seek God Himself through prayer.*

Here's why all of this is so profoundly important – If you are beginning a new leadership role, the very first step to being a healthy, effective leader is tethering your security as a leader to Jesus Christ.

If you've already been leading in a role, it's possible that you may feel the need for a "re-start" or refresh as a leader. I've been there. While already in a leadership role, I came to realize that I needed to deal with my inward fears and finally anchor myself to what God says about me. It made all the difference.

Life and leadership are full of challenges and changes. If we allow ourselves to be tossed and moved by the ups and downs that we all experience in leadership we *will* become weary. Far too often, we take too much of the successes and encouragements we experience in leadership to heart, as well as all of the criticisms and discouragements.

My friend, we must look to the sure anchor. Whatever is happening as we lead, we must be anchored by the truths of who we are in Jesus Christ:

1. I am made by God                    *(Genesis 1:27)*

2. He loved me before I loved Him      *(Romans 5:8)*

3. Nothing can separate me from        *(Romans 8:38–39)*
   His love

4. In Christ, I am completely          *(Romans 3:24)*
   approved of by God

5. I am secure because God always      *(2 Corinthians 1:20)*
   keeps His promises

One of my favorite songs that our church sings on Sunday says, "I'm no longer a slave to fear; I am a child of God."[2] When we are secure as to who we are in Christ, we experience much more freedom as leaders. We recognize that leading well is not about mitigating or deflecting our fears anymore. Rather, leading is an opportunity to be faithful with whatever God has given us, while remembering that who we are in Christ and our future security will never change.

Do not miss this when I say that the different roles we find ourselves in are great places *to add* value, but they are awful places *to find* our value.

From a young age we are taught to seek accolades and acclaim wherever we can. From blue ribbons at the spelling bee, to the honor roll in high school, to hundreds of likes on social media— these are just the beginnings of an appetite for recognition. For some of us, accolades, recognition, and success can be like a drug that we will exhaust ourselves to find more of. To be clear, being recognized for doing well is not a bad thing. It is a good thing! However, we have to keep our appetites in check by recognizing where our true value comes from. When we do, we will feel free to rest, understanding that He holds not only the world, but also our careers, our ministries, and all that we're responsible for in His hands.

## Am I Doing This Right?

Many of us are hands-on learners. We almost need to try before we're given instructions. As we try, we'll often ask someone who might be an expert, "Am I doing this right?" As you've read through this chapter, you may be asking, "Am I doing this right? Am I finding my security in Christ?" While I wish I could say there was a perfect system or metric for measuring this, there is not. However, as we seek to have Christ as our anchor, here are three habits that I would encourage you to pursue on a consistent basis:

### 1. Find Ways to Be Reminded of Who You Are in Christ

The core truths of who we are in Christ are found in God's Word, so we must first look there. Seek and even write out scriptures that speak to the five truths aforementioned in this chapter. Obviously, I've given you a head start by providing some scripture references already.

8

Don't only be in God's Word by yourself. We each need to spend time in community with other Christians who will help keep us grounded as we remind each other of who we are in Christ.

## 2. Ask For The Belief

In Mark 9, a father asks Jesus if there is anything He could do to help or heal his son, and Jesus tells the father, "All things are possible for one who believes." I love the father's response: "I believe; help my unbelief!" Often, we know the truth of what God says about us, but, at the same time, we struggle with believing and need His help to believe. May we never hesitate to ask God to help us believe Him and His Word.

## 3. Do A "Rub Check"

At certain points in leadership we feel tension. I call it *the rub*. It's where we feel a conflict or tension within us because someone or something is *rubbing* against the inward fears we talked about earlier. Different situations create these inward tensions in leaders. Here are a few examples:

- We feel the need to defend ourselves when we are asked why we handled a situation a certain way.

- We feel frustrated and bitter towards a leader of ours who doesn't necessarily buy into our idea of how a project, effort, or strategy should go.

- Someone we lead offers feedback on how we can be a better leader. Instead of considering at least some of their feedback, we completely disregard it and possibly begin to disregard that person.

- When an effort we lead isn't going well, we feel the need to control and micro-manage rather than ask for help.

When we begin to feel tensions such as these, that's when we need to do a *"rub check."*

First, we need to ask ourselves, *"Why am I feeling this way? What is really bothering me here? Is there an inward fear driving my response?"* Then we need to ask, *"As someone who is secure in Christ, what is the best way to both understand and respond to whatever it is that is causing this rub within me?"*

Begin to practice the *rub check*. It's a way of responding as someone who is secure in Christ, rather than someone who is tethered to a faulty anchor.

**Before you start (or restart) the climb as a leader,** know who's holding the other end of your rope. A climber who has a belayer who isn't completely trusted will always be insecure and handicapped by some kind of fear. But a climber who has a belayer who is completely trusted will always climb in freedom. If you and I are going to be healthy, effective leaders we must secure ourselves to Christ. With Him as our solid anchor, we will lead in freedom and find the rest we need.

# Reflection & Discussion Questions

1. What kind of leadership role are you currently in? What are some unique aspects of that role?

2. What are one or two inward fears you have as a leader? What is a *faulty anchor* you might be tempted to cling to?

3. Look again at the five core truths of who we are in Jesus Christ that were listed. Which truth do you think you might struggle to believe the most? Why do you think that is?

4. What is one practical thing you could do that would help you continually be reminded of who you are in Christ?

# Coaching Moment

1. If you have a coach, ask him or her about a specific fear he or she has in leadership and how your coach addresses it. If you don't have a coach, find someone whose leadership you admire and ask if the individual would share a moment when he or she has dealt with fear in leadership. Ask what was learned from the experience.

2. If you are comfortable, share a leadership fear you face. Don't try to varnish it as you talk about it. Listen to how you describe it and pay attention to the feelings you have as you talk about it. What do you think you can learn from this?

# 2

# COACHABLE

In August of 2009, Walt Disney Co. decided to buy Marvel Entertainment.[1] Historically a comic book company, Marvel had recently begun producing its own movies. In the first ten years of owning Marvel Entertainment, Disney made more than $18.2 billion dollars at the global box office alone.[2] Why the success? Clearly, Walt Disney Co. has always been great at telling stories, but now Disney was able to tell stories about heroes. And, as the ticket sales show, people love heroes.

As a child, I was a fan of Batman. For the comic book purists reading this, yes, I do know that Batman is a *DC Comics* character and not a *Marvel* character. Nonetheless, he is a beloved superhero. Batman is different from a lot of superheroes because he doesn't have special powers derived from being born on another planet or from a science experiment gone wrong. What Batman has is resources. Being the orphaned son of a billionaire, Bruce Wayne (Batman's real name) has access to technology, equipment, and training that, combined with his unrelenting courage, make him a great, crime-fighting detective.

But what is Batman's greatest resource? It's not the Batmobile or any of his cool gadgets or gizmos. It's his butler, Alfred Pennyworth, because Alfred is much more than a butler to Bruce Wayne—he is his mentor and guide. Sure, Bruce has incredible skills and talent, but he needs Alfred's wisdom and experience. We see a glimpse of this in the film *The Dark Knight* when Alfred tells Batman:

> *"Endure, Master Wayne. Take it. They'll hate you for it, but that's the point of Batman; he can be the outcast. He can make the choice that no one else can make—the right choice."*[3]

Almost always in the background, Alfred helps to guide and push Bruce to be wiser, to be better, and to do what is right, even when it's difficult. Without Alfred's wisdom, I don't think Bruce would be Batman or, at least, he wouldn't last long as the caped crusader.

## The Hero In The Background

Years ago, I began noticing two trends in conversations with wise, effective leaders. First, they intentionally seek out knowledge and wisdom. Second, they've had one or more heroes in the background who have played an integral part in their growth as leaders. I call these heroes *coaches*.

A friend of mine, who worked as the COO for one of the twelve US Federal Reserve banks, shared a story from his beginning time in the banking world. His supervisor recognized the talent my friend had but also the areas where he needed to grow and develop. His supervisor offered to meet with him for an hour *every day* to coach him, but there were two expectations that came along with it.

First, because of the supervisor's schedule, they would have to meet very early in the morning before most arrived to the office. Second, if my friend showed up late once then it would be the end of their coaching arrangement.

But he did it. He showed up early, every day to be coached, and today he, too, is educating emerging bankers as well as providing consulting services from his own consulting group.

Another friend of mine worked as the CEO of a well-known para-church ministry and is currently an Executive Director for another Christian company. In our conversations around leadership, she shared with me about a mentor who was willing to coach her, even if it meant having difficult conversations and telling her truths that might've been hard to hear. Her coach was able to say, "This is what I'm seeing" and helped her understand how she could be a better leader. These wise coaches, who are willing to be honest with us for our benefit, are a gift.

This friend now travels the country to help coach and equip ministry leaders.

What was the key for both of these leaders? It wasn't only that they had coaches but that they, as new leaders, were **coachable**—they were willing to be taught, challenged, and led.

Starting well in leadership requires this kind of posture. Often, we might begin with a breadth of zeal, courage, and confidence, but the depth of our understanding might be limited by our experience. For some of us, our natural tendency is to prove that we know better or at least make it look like we do, even when we don't. Sometimes this can be a mask for deep insecurity. If we aren't careful, we might overcompensate for our insecurities by building a façade of false confidence.

Most often, seasoned leaders see right through this. And almost always, those who lead us aren't looking for us to fake it. What I've seen from the most seasoned leaders is they'd rather see a new leader (or an experienced leader in a new role or context) have the self-awareness to know that it's an opportunity for them to be coached.

Know that it is OK to not know everything. Leaders are lifelong learners.

Christian leader, whatever role, context, or season of leadership we're in, we *all* need coaching. We all have room for growth and development, and we will all face new challenges. If we aren't facing new challenges, then we aren't moving forward in our leadership. And to move forward, we need to employ the following three habits of the coachable leader…

## Can You Be Taught?

Teaching and instruction are core activities that cultivate development. A societal norm, there are people and systems in place to teach and instruct us. In our earliest years our parents begin to put up boundaries and expectations for where to play, how to play, and what kinds of things are safe to be played with. Then we enter our places of education: schools, homeschools, and now online schools. Our entire lives, there are teachers and influencers available to us. The catch, however, is that it's up to us to maintain a posture in which we are teachable.

The book of Proverbs discusses this idea that those who are wise are willing to learn, as shown in verse 1:5: "Let the wise *hear* and increase in learning, and the one who understands obtain guidance." This Hebrew word for *hear* (*shama'*) means to hear with attention and interest in order to understand and give heed to (obey).[4] Did you catch that? Teachable leaders don't just listen—they *hear*. They still themselves to understand and not just to retain information but to apply it. For the Christian leader to grow in knowledge, we must learn to *hear* well.

Learning to hear well not only gives us wisdom for today, but it will also gift us wisdom in the future. As Proverbs 19:20 says, "Listen to advice and accept instruction, that you may gain wisdom in the future."

Hearing well can be a struggle, especially since we live in the day of Google. If we have a math problem, we can Google a calculator or formula. If we aren't sure about world events, geography, and or the lyrics to our new favorite song, we can Google the answer. However, this doesn't apply to leadership. We can't just Google the answers to our leadership questions. So, we must build up our cache of knowledge as we're taught.

As leaders we can't and won't always be prepared for every leadership question and challenge that we will face. This is why having a coach is so valuable. The more we are teachable now and able to *hear* to understand, the more likely we are to gain wisdom in the future as we are given opportunities to apply the knowledge we've been taught.

## Can You Be Challenged?

In leadership we will be challenged. People will challenge us, our decisions, our style—among a myriad of other things. While we should be humble enough to realize we can learn from anyone, we should also be diligent enough to not give everyone permission to have a significant voice in our lives and leadership.

Being challenge-able does not mean we invite or receive challenge from every person. *It means we receive challenge well from the right people.* It means inviting wise people to speak into our lives and leadership, because the right people are *for* us and want to see us do well.

The truth of the matter is that not everybody is *for* you. But there will be those who are. So, who are those "for you" people? You might want to consider the following:

- Who is the wise person (or people) in your life and leadership who is willing to invest in you, even if it means some sacrifice on his or her part?

- Who is the person (or people) who is willing to challenge you, to *push back* on your thinking or decision-making, knowing it will make you better equipped as a leader?

- Do you give this wise person permission to ask what you need to be asked and say what you need to hear? Do you still and quiet yourself to understand?

We often don't like to be uncomfortable, but some pressure and some heat often result in a more solid leader.

## Can You Be Led?

If you and I can't be led ourselves, then we have no business leading other people.

There are no perfect leaders. When we lead, we are asking others to follow us, fully knowing we will not lead them perfectly. We're asking them to live with the shortcomings of our leadership. We are, whether we realize it or not, asking them to extend grace to us. And if you and I can't extend this same grace to our leaders, then it doesn't make much sense to expect this grace from those whom we lead.

Please don't misunderstand me. When I speak of extending grace, I'm not talking about looking the other way when someone clearly has undermined their role, whatever the case may be: sin, misconduct, gross mismanagement, etc. That is not grace. That is passivity. I am saying that, as leaders, we need to have enough self-awareness to know that if we're asking others to follow us and live in the reality that we're imperfect leaders, we'd better be willing to do the same for those who are tasked with leading us.

# Where Do I Look?

Maybe you're reading this chapter and realize you don't have a coach—somebody who can speak into your leadership to help you grow. Maybe you're asking: *Where should I look? What should I look for?* I'm glad that you asked! Here are four coach-finding tips for you:

**1. Look for somebody who has more experience in the role or a role that's similar to the one you're in**

Oftentimes these coaches might already be in our church, organization, or company. But if they're not, many times these places will be connected to resources or networks that will have those people. We just need to seek them out.

When I was a Student Pastor, I desperately wanted to grow in wisdom for discipling students. (If you don't know, "discipling" is a term for helping others to follow Jesus.) So, what did I do? *I sat around and figured it all out by myself.* NOPE! I reached out to the national youth director for our church's denomination. Not only did he spend some personal time investing in me, he also connected me with a guy, Mark, who had experience discipling students and was willing to coach me. Mark and I spent six straight weeks on coaching calls (shout out to the folks at Skype!), and he coached me through material that would help me better disciple students. At the end of those six weeks, I'd been coached enough to where I took that material and began coaching some of our own adult youth leaders and high school students, enabling them to have more wisdom when it came to helping students follow Jesus. All of that was a result of two simple things: a coachable posture and a phone call.

## 2. Have a plan

Notice that Mark and I had a plan about his coaching. We decided early on that we were going to meet weekly over the course of six weeks and discuss the material he recommended.

Your coaching plan may or may not be similar to ours. Either way, it's important to have a plan with your coach. For instance, some of us have supervisors who are our coaches, and we'll include coaching time during a regular, standing meeting schedule. That is great! Keep doing that! For others, we'll lean on other people to be coaches, and we'll have to configure a plan. In this case, I highly recommend defining two things:

**Define the focus.** What is it that you will talk about/meet over? This will guard you both from spending the time discussing things that are not a priority.

**Define the time.** What will be the amount of time you'll meet (i.e. for an hour)? What will be the frequency you'll meet (weekly? every other week? monthly?) and over how long of a timeframe (i.e. over the course of three months)?

Defining the focus and time will help both you and your coach know that there is a goal and an end. This will help you to be more diligent, disciplined, and prepared to use the time wisely.

## 3. As much as you can, seek out a *Christian* coach

If you're a leader in a church or ministry this goes without saying. But often in the marketplace there are people in our field who have a lot of wisdom but don't share our Christian worldview and beliefs. Remember that they, too, are made in the image of God, and their giftedness and skill reflect His grace in their lives, whether they realize it or not. If you decide to have a coachable posture towards them, then I recommend having a supplemental Christian voice (or voices) in your life who has experience as a Christian in the market-place. This supplemental voice can help keep you grounded to the reliable anchor as you labor and lead.

## 4. Let the coach lead

It can often be difficult to ask leaders to be led. For many of us, it is often not our natural tendency to wait or to let others guide. Yet, when we ask somebody for their time and effort in order to coach us and help us grow, we would be wise to heed Proverbs 1:5 and to *hear* —we must still our-selves with attention in order to understand. This is nearly impossible to do if we are the ones who speak first or most. Sometimes we leaders need to help ourselves get out of our own way.

Start well by allowing leaders to lead you.

# Reflection & Discussion Questions

1. In your own words, what does a coachable leader look like?

2. Who is somebody in your life who has already made a positive impact on your life and leadership by being willing to teach, challenge, or lead you?

3. If you don't have a coach, who is an experienced leader you might approach? If you can't think of anyone, what network or resource could you utilize to find a coach?

# Coaching Moment

1. Ask your coach to share about a leader who made a positive impact on him or her. What was one, valuable lesson he or she learned from that leader?

2. Consider the three habits of coachable leaders (they can be taught, challenged, and led). Share which habit you believe comes most naturally to you. Is there a habit you might struggle with? As you share, what can you learn about yourself?

# 3

# HAVE THE END IN MIND

Every Christmas season Charles Dickens' fictional work *A Christmas Carol* is revisited through countless film and television adaptations. A literary classic, it's very difficult to find someone who won't recognize Ebenezer Scrooge as the ruthless, uncompassionate businessman who is visited by three spirits on Christmas Eve or his famous line, "Bah! Humbug!"

During this famous story, the turning point takes place when the Ghost of Christmas Yet to Come reveals to Scrooge the day when he no longer lives. It is here that he comes face-to-face with his legacy—the enduring effect of his presence on the lives of others—and he is horrified by the results. For the first time, Scrooge is made aware of the damage caused by his cruelty and selfishness and begins to plead with the Ghost for the opportunity to change his legacy.

As the tale ends, Scrooge awakes on Christmas morning and realizes he has, indeed, been given a second chance. Now, having clarity for the kind of legacy he desires to leave, Scrooge, "became as good a friend, as good a master, and as good a man, as the good old city knew, or any other good old city, town, or borough, in the good old world."[1]

Wherever we are, Christian leaders must remember to have the end in mind. In other words, we must be thoughtful, intentional, and prayerful as to the kind of **legacy** we want to leave.

Pause and think for a moment about where God has you right now: the church, company, or organization you're with. Have you been there for some time or are you just beginning? What kind of role are you in? Who are the people you "rub shoulders with" on a regular basis? With all that in mind, know that one day all of that will change. There will be an end to that season of leadership.

However, while that season will end, the legacy you leave can last.

Christian leaders must ask themselves, *"What enduring effect do I hope to have left on the people God surrounded me with?"* This question is paramount for any leader because it will shape both the "why" and the "how" of all that we do.

## The Why & The How

A few years ago I had the opportunity to partner with a handful of professional football players in an outreach event for local youth and their families. The players shared about their lives as professional athletes, life with their families, and also how they live out their faith in Christ. One of them ended up being featured on a hit television show that highlights a different team as they prepare for the upcoming season during training camp.

This particular player was a captain and leader on the team. At the beginning of training camp, he stood up in front his teammates and asked them to consider their "*Why.*" He encouraged them to think about and reflect on why they were there. What was going to drive them as they labored and endured the heat, sweat, and bruising of training camp? He challenged them to write down their "*Why*" and keep it somewhere they would see it often to be reminded often of the ultimate purpose of those days.[2]

Christian leader—what is your "*Why*" for leading others?

There is a common misconception when it comes to legacies. We far too often associate legacies with endings. The reality is, however, that *legacies don't begin where something ends; they begin when something starts.* The first day you show up and are present with people is when your legacy begins to be cultivated. And each day you are present helps shape that legacy. I would contend that the more thoughtful we are about our legacy then the more intentional we'll be in our daily leadership.

Our leadership habits leave an imprint on people's lives. These habits include the ways we respond to, interact with, and lead others. The seemingly small, consistent interactions we have really do matter. Surely there will be days when we are faced with more impactful decisions and heavier situations. Yet I am convinced that how we navigate the big decisions and weighty situations often mirror how we consistently handle the seemingly small ones.

## A Better Story

Consider Peter, one of Jesus' disciples. When we read the Gospels, we see that while he often had great faith, Peter also had his shortcomings. He had a bad habit of not keeping his emotions in check. He also seemed to be a little overconfident in himself.

Peter's shortcomings came to a head when Jesus was betrayed and arrested. As Jesus was put on trial by the local religious leaders, Peter waited outside, keeping warm near a fire in the courtyard. When he was recognized as one of Jesus' followers by others there, Peter had the opportunity to show the courage and fortitude he always tried to convey. Instead, he showed he had little courage and reacted in fear — denying his friend and teacher.

Despite Peter's shortcomings, God's grace was sufficient to write a better story and legacy for Peter than he could have written himself or by his own will. Jesus restored Peter, and He would use him as an impactful, effective leader in the early church.

That same grace that was available for Peter is available to write a better story and legacy for us as well. For the Christian leader, we must recognize that our legacy cannot and should not be ultimately driven by our own activity or vision. Rather, we must recognize two realities when it comes to the legacy of a Christian leader:

## 1. **Our legacy will be shaped by God's Activity.**

For Christian leaders, we must reject the cultural narrative that our lives and legacy can somehow be completely driven and shaped by our own efforts and willpower. Herein lies the paradoxical nature of the Christian life. While we are responsible for the habits and decisions of our lives and leadership, we also recognize that "the heart of man plans his way, but the Lord establishes his steps" (Proverbs 16:9). In the midst of our own activity, God Himself is active, working the different facets of our lives for purposes greater than our own.

If we give in to the world's false narrative that we somehow must will our lives and legacy, then we are susceptible to consistently leading out of the fear that we won't get it right. Instead, we can lead with courage as we recognize our role is to be faithful to the place and time God has placed us and to trust Him and His activity.

Recognizing the reality of God's activity also guards us from the great enemy of the healthy leader: *pride*. The man or woman who believes, albeit subconsciously, that success as a leader is the result of his or her own doing has no need for God. For the Christian leader, is there a more dangerous mindset to have? But when we recognize God's activity in our lives, we realize that even our best work as leaders is ultimately because of His activity.

## 2. **Our legacy will last as much as it benefits and extends God's Kingdom.**

Let's turn our attention to another Christmas story—one that actually did happen. When Jesus came to earth 2,000 years ago, as fully man and fully God, something significant changed in the history of humanity. Jesus came as *Immanuel*, God with us. During His earthly ministry He proclaimed that the Kingdom of God was now at hand.

But what is the Kingdom of God? It is the future reality that God has established for His people. Revelation 21:3 speaks to this future reality when it says, "Behold, the dwelling place of God is with man. He will dwell with them, and they will be his people, and God himself will be with them as their God." This is the endgame for the whole of human history: God's redeemed people finally living the lives they were meant to live with Him, in perfect peace, joy, and harmony with each other and with creation. While we don't yet live in the time where this Kingdom is fully realized, the realities of God's Kingdom are piercing into history now.

God has called His people to live as citizens and ambassadors of this future Kingdom today. As citizens of His Kingdom, we are called to live out the Kingdom realities that Jesus taught, including those of grace, mercy, and justice. As we do, He gives us opportunities as ambassadors to invite those who are strangers and aliens (like we once were) to receive the redemption, transformation, and Kingdom citizenship that come only through the person and work of Jesus Christ—*Immanuel,* God with us.

Herein lies what I believe must be the primary driver of our legacy if we want one that lasts: *Our legacies must be Kingdom legacies.* For our legacy will last only as much as it benefits and extends God's Kingdom.

## Kingdom Vision Shapes Kingdom Leadership

Our vision for a Kingdom legacy must shape the why and how of our leadership. Knowing the future that is already promised can and should drive us in the heat, sweat, and bruising of leadership. The values of God's Kingdom can and should shape healthy habits that bring God glory as we interact with and lead others.

This applies to every Christian leader whom God has given a position of influence, not just church leaders. God can and will use the daily habits, interactions, and decisions of the Christian executive of a Fortune 500 company to shape and mold a legacy that benefits and extends His Kingdom. God can do the same with the local business owner or school administrator. But every Christian leader must begin with the end in mind. We must have vision for the kind of Kingdom legacy we want to leave and then pray like crazy for God's activity and for His Kingdom to be benefited and extended.

## The Legacy Of A Friend

During the Great Depression of the early 1930s, a young woman by the name of Mary was the only individual in her small, Italian family who was able to find work. During a troubled time for so many, Mary found herself facing the pressure to keep up her job at a local business just so her family could survive.

In the midst of this difficult and immense pressure, a kind, young female co-worker befriended Mary. Every day she would greet Mary with a smile, talk with her, and encourage her. As their friendship grew, this young woman invited Mary to join her in reading the Bible on lunch breaks and during other times they could meet together. As Mary read the pages and was helped to understand what they said, her eyes were opened to the Gospel of Jesus Christ. Mary responded by trusting in Jesus. And, while Mary didn't know it at the time, her friend's impact on her life would affect generations.

Mary would go on to marry a handsome, young man named Dominic. He was called to be a pastor at a local church in their city. For decades he could be heard singing on Sundays, leading congregational songs from the hymnal – often in Italian. They served their local church faithfully for years and raised their children with a foundation of faith in Jesus Christ. They would have children, grandchildren, great grandchildren, and they have great, great grandchildren living today. Every generation of their family has been impacted by the Gospel in one way or another…and it all started with an intentional friend from work.

How do I know all this about Mary and her family? Because Mary is and was my great-grandmother. It has been some years since she has gone home to be with Jesus, and I miss her dearly. To this day, her faith in Christ impacts my life and now my children's lives.

I wish I knew the name of the young woman who befriended my great-grandmother and introduced her to

Christ, all those years ago. But I can tell you that I am eternally grateful for her and the enduring effect her life continues to have on every generation of my family.

Friends – that is a *Kingdom legacy*.

## Reflection & Discussion Questions

1. What do you think a *Kingdom* legacy looks like?

2. What gifts or abilities has God given you that can make a difference for others?

3. How does awareness of God's activity bring us both courage and humility?

## Coaching Moment

1. Ask your coach if he or she feels comfortable sharing his or her "Why." Ask what inspires them to keep leading faithfully, even on the most difficult days. Where have they seen or sensed God's activity in their leadership journey?

2. Share with your coach what motivates you to want to be in leadership. Is there a way you have sensed God's activity in your leadership journey to this point? If so, share about that with your coach.

# 4

# TIME TO BE SHERLOCK

I recently had lunch with a friend who shared with me that he was a candidate for a promotion at the large, well-known retail company he works for. Job changes and opportunities for promotion happen all the time, but I couldn't help feel an extra sense of joy for this particular friend. While we'd had lunch a number of times before this, some of those lunches didn't always have the same, positive vibe that this one did.

Not so long ago my friend went through a difficult job transition. When he had first mentioned his troubles at work, I'd offered to get together and offer a third-party perspective. As he shared his work dilemma, I came to realize that he had a made a simple, yet significant mistake at his place of employment.

Understand that my friend is a very sharp, gifted, and driven person. In his previous job of leasing and managing properties, his sales numbers were clearly outperforming those of his peers. But while there were explicit expectations for his sales performance, there were also implicit expectations for how he should work as part of his team. Unfortunately, my friend had been so driven that he had little relationship with his teammates and had not done enough to be part of the collaborative and supportive culture at work. His failing to intentionally understand the culture and implied values of his team combined with his supervisor's lack of leadership and communication created a chasm too wide to overcome.

## A Community With A Culture

Whenever we join a church, company, or organization we are stepping into a *community*, and every community has a *culture*. Whether you find yourself in a small business, large firm, young church plant, century-old church, new small group, or well-known non-profit, there is a culture to be investigated and understood. The word "culture" comes from the Latin *cultura*, meaning "to cultivate." Over time an organization's history, language, and values are cultivated by its people. The result is **organizational culture**. For the Christian leader to start well, we must seek to understand the culture of the community we are stepping into.

Anyone who joins a community and doesn't understand its culture will struggle to assimilate. They will most likely find themselves frustrated as well as frustrating others. I know from personal experience. I have stepped into staff teams at churches and didn't take the time or effort to understand the history and values of the church, its people, or the team I was part of. I quickly alienated good people and lost trust with superiors because it was clear that I was operating out of assumptions and not thoughtfully understanding the people I was trying to lead.

Years ago, I stepped into a new role leading a local church ministry after serving on a leadership team at another church.

The previous church placed a very high value on larger group gatherings centered around engaging teaching and corporate worship that featured high quality production (sound, lights, etc.).

When I stepped into my new leadership role at the next church, I did not start well. One reason was that I often led and made decisions based on things that mattered for the culture of where I used to be, rather than where I was. I spent a lot of time (and budget) updating our gathering space, production equipment, and reworking the format of our gathering times to be more about high production value.

Here was the problem though: In the culture of that church, few cared much about any of that. You know what they did value? Relationships and care through effective small groups. Was it important for us to have quality sound equipment and a projector that worked? Sure. Should I have prioritized much more time and effort into building relationships, as well as helping to cultivate awesome and excellent small groups? Most definitely.

Early on I spent a lot of time on things that didn't matter much to the people I had the opportunity to serve. While it was never my intention, in those early days I probably came off as a pretty obtuse leader. Why? I didn't take time to understand the culture.

I have seen great, gifted, sharp people experience the same difficulties in joining a new organization. This includes people who already have leadership experience. Sometimes even seasoned leaders forget that a new place is still a new place, a new people are still new a people, and, as such, they need to be understood.

During His earthly ministry Jesus had a clear understanding of the people around him and their culture. He knew their history. He knew how to speak their language in ways they could understand. He also knew what they valued. Now, you and I do not have the gift of omniscience (being all-knowing) that Jesus has, so in order to follow His example we have to become culture detectives.

## Culture Detective

People love mysteries. The genre of mystery books, television shows, and films brings in billions of dollars every year. There is a thrill in the journey of joining the hero, such as the famous detective Sherlock Holmes, as he searches for clues. These detectives employ the skills of making observations and asking good questions to solve their cases, and we must do the same in our own organizations.

### 1. Making Observations

The best culture detectives take the time to observe in order to understand their organization. The most significant *tell* of an organization's culture will always be its people. Consider the language that people use, the style in which they work and interact with one another, and the things they celebrate. I suggest observing the organizational leaders first and then look to others. More often than not, the values of leadership become the values of the organization.

In addition, take time to observe the look and feel of the facilities and signage on the walls. Look at the organization's presence online and on social media. Consider what people wear. Observe these things, not for the sake of making assumptions or arriving at conclusions about people, but to increase your understanding of the community you are part of. As you observe, ask yourself, "What might these things mean or say about what matters to the people here?"

### 2. Asking Good Questions

As a younger leader I felt a self-imposed pressure to prove myself, my leadership, and my competency. This resulted in spending a lot of time trying to help other people understand me and all of my ideas. In his book, *The 7 Habits of Highly Effective People*, Stephen Covey implores his readers to seek first to understand, then to be understood.[1] Looking back on my early days of leadership, I wish I would have had the humility and wisdom to have asked more questions. I also wish I would have spent less time making statements or giving my opinions.

Effective culture detectives genuinely want to understand the people they're with. They ask good questions and then quiet themselves so they can hear, observe, and learn. Here are some examples:

| Seeking to Be Understood | Seeking to Understand |
| --- | --- |
| "This is the way I am…" | "How can I best work with you?" |
| "I'm of the opinion that…" | "What have you learned that could help me?" |
| "I think we should do it this way…" | "Why do you think this is the best way?" |
| "I don't like doing this…" | "Could you help me find a way to do this better?" |

Please don't misunderstand me—I'm not saying that those new to an organization can never share their thoughts, opinions, or suggestions. I am saying, however, that until we take the time to genuinely understand the place and people we're with, then our opinions will most likely be misinformed and fall on deaf ears.

## The Culture Puzzle

Organizational culture is like a puzzle. There are a lot of different pieces that, at first glance, may seem a bit random, disjointed, and somewhat overwhelming. However, as we take the time to understand these pieces, we'll begin to see the big picture a bit clearer. And as we navigate our community's culture, we'll recognize and understand its history, language, and values.

**History.** People's experiences always have a key role in shaping their hopes, goals, and even their fears. It is no different for an organization. Knowing the history and being sensitive to it will help us to understand why certain expectations, practices, and policies are in place. It will also help us avoid possible landmines, where we unintentionally "step on" people's fears, frustrations, and even past failures. Often, a church or company's policies can be traced back to a problem of the past. As a friend of mine puts it, "Policies are the scar tissue of an organization."

**Language.** Every place has its own language and a good culture detective will learn it. Within this language will be certain buzzwords and phrases that should not only be known, but also understood within the context of that organization.

For example, every church where I've been on staff talks about *outreach*. It is almost always a buzzword. Yet what outreach means and looks like can and is often vastly different at different churches. At one church where I worked, outreach meant primarily planning and hosting events for church members to invite nonbelieving friends to. At another, outreach meant going and meeting the physical needs of the marginalized. While it's the same word, it has a vastly different meaning depending on the context and culture of an organization.

**Stated Values.** Nowadays it is easy to find an organization's stated values. Almost always they will be posted on a website somewhere, or when you walk into their offices, there might be signs on the wall with a mission statement. When we become part of an organization we now represent that organization. As representatives (and as leaders) we have a responsibility to know and practice the stated values of our organization.

**Implied Values.** Remember my friend who went through that difficult job transition? What was the cause? He was not aware of the implied values of team collaboration and support in their sales efforts. There is a good chance that this expectation was nowhere to be found on their company website or stated in his onboarding, yet it was a high value to his team.

Clearly, organizations and their leaders always have implied values. These are expectations that won't be found in a document but are communicated through language, celebration, and sometimes correction. They can be easily overlooked because over time (and the longer people have been with an organization) people may not realize these implicit values even exist.

## Learn The Culture

When we join an organization, we're joining a community, and communities are full of people.

If we want to lead anyone, we must meet people where they are, in their culture. And if we want to understand that culture, then it's time to be Sherlock.

Being a culture detective takes time, patience, and intentionality. Good culture detectives seek to understand before being understood. They make observations and ask good questions. They learn and respect an organization's history and its people's experiences. They learn the language. They learn the values.

Above all, they seek to understand before being understood.

# Reflection & Discussion Questions

1. Why is it important to understand an organization's culture?

2. What kinds of things would you observe to better understand an organization's culture? What are examples of good questions you might ask?

3. Think about the church, company, or organization you are currently part of. What are some unique aspects of its culture? *Consider its history, language, and values.*

4. When was a time when you forged ahead without understanding the culture or observed someone else who did? What did you learn from it?

# Coaching Moment

1. Ask your coach to share a time when navigating the culture didn't go well. What happened? What did he or she learn? If your coach could go back and give some advice, what would it be?

2. Share with your coach one, unique aspect of the culture of your organization. Being aware of that, what might it look like for you navigate that aspect of the culture well?

# 5

# WHO AM I?

Let's play a little game.

I am a large cat. I have spots. I am incredibly fast. *Who Am I?*

I'm a nanny. I enjoy a good, spoonful of sugar. I leave when the winds change. *Who Am I?*

I'm very polite. I wear sweaters. I'd like for you to be my neighbor. *Who Am I?*

*Who Am I?* is a simple but fun game. It's also somewhat mind-blowing. The idea that we can mention only a few character traits and others can specifically name a thing or person out of the millions of objects, creatures, or people who have existed on this planet and throughout history is incredible. God designed our minds to be truly brilliant. We have the capacity to take bits of information and use them to construct a whole in our minds of what something or someone is to us. In the end, all these little traits are brought together to distinguish a thing, creature, or person.

This game should also make us pause and wonder, *What distinguishes me?* A good place to look is our character. In fact, the Merriam-Webster Dictionary defines **character** as, "one of the attributes or features that make up and distinguish an individual."[1]

While there are a lot of different things that can distinguish an individual leader, the most important is our character. Christian leader—*Who are you?* In other words, how does your *character* distinguish you?

## Character According To Proverbs

Throughout the twelfth chapter of Proverbs we see a comparison between the good character of the wise person and the bad character of the fool. Look at some of these ways they are distinguished:

| *The Wise* | *The Fool* | |
|---|---|---|
| Desires to learn and be taught | Refuses to receive teaching or correction | v.1 |
| Has good sense | Thinks twistedly | v. 8 |
| Considers the advice of others | Always thinks they are right | v. 15 |
| Speaks the truth | Is deceitful | v. 17 |
| Helps cultivate peace | Causes conflict | v. 20 |
| Is prudent | Is slothful and lazy | v. 24 |
| Helps their neighbor | Leads others astray | v. 26 |
| Their way leads to life | Their way leads to death | v. 28 |

For the Christian leader, our character matters. It not only matters personally for our lives and leadership, but Proverbs

12 helps us to see that our character also matters because it leaves an imprint on the lives of others.

In August of 1963, 250,000 people gathered in front of the Lincoln Memorial to draw attention to the inequality and challenges that African Americans were still facing even a century after President Abraham Lincoln gave his famous Emancipation Proclamation. Known as the March on Washington, this would be the gathering in which Christian minister and American Civil Rights leader Dr. Martin Luther King Jr. would give his famed "I Have A Dream" speech. I have heard this address dozens of times, and upon each hearing there is one portion of it that always resonates with me:

*"I have a dream that my four little children will one day live in a nation where they will not be judged by the color of their skin but by the content of their character. I have a dream today."*

In the proceeding lines, Dr. King would challenge the character of George Wallace, the governor of Alabama at the time. Wallace was known for being a staunch racist and segregationist and for leading others to champion the oppressive Jim Crow laws. King would then add,

*"One day right there in Alabama little black boys and black girls will be able to join hands with little white boys and white girls as sisters and brothers. I have a dream today."*[2]

Many of the good character traits of Dr. King left an imprint on the lives of so many. Unfortunately, so did the poor character traits of George Wallace. While you and I may not have the platforms that these leaders had, if we are wise we will learn from the teachings of history and see that the character of every leader matters. What does this mean for us? The stakes are too high for us not to pay attention to our character.

# The Worst (& Best) Lunch Ever

Looking back at my time as a new leader, one of my greatest regrets is the utter lack of attention I gave to my character. When I reflect on some of the ugly moments in my life and leadership, I (with the benefit of hindsight) clearly see my lack of good character, which, frankly, makes me shudder.

I think about the thoughtless things I've said and the quick, rude ways I said them. I think about my posture of arrogance and self-centeredness. I think about the times I was deceitful in order to make myself look better. These are just the tip of the iceberg. And it makes my stomach churn.

While my regret is very real, so is my gratitude. I'm grateful for the people whom God placed in my life who were patient with me. I can think of folks who took the time to pull me aside, ask tough questions, and say tough truths. Too often I listened but didn't *hear* or *heed* what these true friends were saying. But at a certain point, things had to change. In particular, my character had to change. And what caused this sudden attention to my character? Pain.

Years ago, I had a seminary professor share this gem of truth with me: *Until the pain of staying the same is greater than the pain of change, people prefer to stay the same.*

My consistent lack of attention to my character was causing me way too much pain. Even more, it was causing pain and frustration for others.

I'll never forget the worst (and best) lunch that helped to change the trajectory of my leadership. My supervisor and mentor at the time invited me out to eat. Little did I know he had some tough truths to tell me that day about my character. As we sat together, he began by asking questions and giving examples of my character traits and habits that concerned him. (This included those that I mentioned earlier.) He shared observations that were painful to hear. He said what he needed to say with clarity but also with grace and kindness.

Throughout our conversation, my mentor's counsel was not, "Chris, you need to fix this." Rather, his counsel was, "Chris, you need to go to the Lord and ask Him to open your eyes. You need Him to show you what is going on in your heart that is causing you to act and respond in these ways that aren't healthy."

At the end of our conversation, it was apparent that the stakes were high for me and for the people I was responsible to. I realized that the road of the leadership journey only extends as far as one's character allows it. And I was quickly approaching a dead end.

God used my pain, including this conversation with my supervisor and mentor, to make me desperate for transformation that could only come from Him. What would take place over the following months was a process of prayer, repentance, and seeking godly counsel.

God graciously helped me see that I had become very selfish and self-centered. He revealed some of my inward fears and how those drove me to not be honest with myself, not take responsibility for my own actions, and even justify my own immaturity. He also healed some hurts and wounds that I'd experienced, even from as far back as high school.

For the first time in a long time, I actually possessed some semblance of pliability and a teachable spirit that weren't there before. Those I worked with, as well as the team I led, began to notice. Not surprisingly, the trajectory of my leadership began to change, not because of an increase of information but because of a character transformation.

I share this story with you not because I am foolish enough to believe that I've arrived on some peak on the mountain of character development. Honestly, I often sense that more than ever there is an overwhelming amount of God's transforming work needed in my life and that I have barely started the climb. Rather, I share this story with the hope that others will avoid being a fool in the way I was, giving little or no attention to my character. I also share it so that you will know the true source of good character.

## The Source of Good Character

Culturally we give ourselves too much credit when it comes to character development. Consider the frequency of self-help books that are released. Unfortunately, many of these are promoted under the guise of a kind of pseudo-Christianity. Consider their sales and popularity—it's easy to surmise that far too many of us think we can will ourselves towards better character. Even on social media, when bad character is revealed by the actions of others, we often see people admonishing others to *#BeBetter*. The Gospel truth is that, on our own, we can't.

In Psalm 139:23-24, David asks this of God:

Search me, O God, and know my heart!
Try me and know my thoughts!
And see if there be any grievous way in me,
and lead me in the way everlasting!

The true source of good character is found in the transforming work of God.

David models this for us in this simple, yet necessary prayer. Good character is found in the humble posture of seeking God and asking Him to make us more pliable and moldable. It's asking Him to search the depth of us—our hearts and thoughts, including that which we can't see and recognize for ourselves. It's asking Him to reveal and deal with the things in us and in our character that grieve Him. It's asking Him to show us His way. It's recognizing we don't have the means to go God's way on our own, and only He can transform and empower us towards it. And as He transforms us, we'll become more and more of our "new self" as our character increasingly reflects the character of our Creator.

**Christian leaders, we must pay attention to our character.** The road of our leadership will only extend as far as our character allows it. In order to lead others anywhere, we must first lead ourselves to the foot of the throne of God where we are continually asking Him to shape and mold us. To do so, we must have some sense of desperation for the transforming work of God in our lives because only He can make us truly pliable. It is here where our question of *Who am I?* will shift to *Who is God shaping me to be?*

# Reflection & Discussion Questions

1. In what ways does the character of a leader leave an "imprint" on those he or she leads?

2. How would you translate David's prayer Psalm 139:23-24 into your own words? Consider how that might be a consistent prayer for you.

3. What are some of the different ways God transforms our character? What or who might He use as part of His transforming work in our lives?

# Coaching Moment

1. Ask your coach, if he or she feels comfortable sharing a time or situation that was an opportunity for personal growth. Ask your coach what he or she has learned or how he or she has grown in that area.

2. Share with your coach one aspect of your character (that God is still transforming) that you believe, left unchecked, might undermine your leadership. When someone you trust brings this area to light, what would be a healthy way for you to respond?

# 6

# EXCELLENCE

There was once a large, dying tree that sat in my neighbor's yard. It was near our property line, and every time a storm came through fallen tree limbs would litter both my neighbor's yard and ours. I think our neighbor had enough of cleaning up all those limbs, so he decided to hire somebody to cut it down. I also think he was concerned about the safety of our young children if they were ever near the tree on a windy day. He was a good neighbor in that way, and I was thankful for his and his wife's generosity in having it removed.

On the day the tree was to be cut down, I came home from work and noticed that while much of it was gone, about ten feet of the tree trunk still remained. I asked my neighbor when the trunk would be removed as well, and he looked at me, grinned, and said that he had hired a tree carver to turn that stump into an eagle.

As he shared his plan for the stump with me, concerned thoughts ran through my mind: "Oh no, we're going to have a 10-foot-tall eagle next to our property? What if we become known as the house in the neighborhood next to the weird statue? Is he talking about a totem pole? Maybe we could just move instead? I wonder how busy our realtor is right now...." When my neighbor finished sharing, I lied through a forced smile and said, "That sounds like a wonderful idea."

A few days later, an old pickup truck and trailer showed up in front of my neighbor's home. A man stepped out in tattered clothing and with a cigarette in his mouth, and he began pulling chainsaws from the trailer. Before I got in my car to head to work, I went over to introduce myself to the man that we will call Gus.

He may have looked a little gruff, but Gus was incredibly pleasant in how he interacted and spoke with this nosy neighbor who probably should have been minding his own business. I asked a couple, simple questions about his carving business, and I think he could tell I was a little concerned. He politely shared that he had won some awards for excellence in his wood carvings and gave me a web address to check out some of his work. Not surprisingly, looking up that website was the very first thing I did when I arrived at the office that morning.

Gus wasn't joking about the excellence of his work. On his very simple website, Gus had pictures of beautiful wood carvings, both at people's homes and at places of business. He had a piece at one of the premier golf courses in the area and another at a children's hospital. I quickly came to realize that Gus was excellent at what he did and that I needn't be as concerned as I was.

The eventual tree-stump-turned-eagle did receive a lot of notoriety and attention, but not because it looked weird or odd. Gus used his skills of wood-carving as well as wood-burning to turn that tree stump into a beautiful, realistic-looking eagle sitting proudly on top of a shield with a sash around it. It was incredible, like something you would see at a country club.

All summer, folks from around our neighborhood came to see the eagle and take pictures of it. On a regular basis I would ask my wife, "Honey, who are those people outside on our street?" She would respond, "Oh, they're probably just out there looking at the eagle." Even a local news station stopped by to do an interest piece on what Gus had made with his hands. The work of the artist was truly excellent.

## Where Excellence Begins

The term "excellence" is a buzzword that is often used in churches and organizations, but what do we mean by it? I love this definition: **excellence** is doing the best you can with what you have.[1] For someone like Gus, he used his skills and tools to make the best wood carvings he could. In this way, he was excellent.

While defining excellence isn't difficult, practicing excellence takes diligence and discipline. I'm sure that Gus worked diligently at his craft of wood-carving, and that it took lots of discipline to develop it. Christian leaders must also develop habits of excellence in everything they do, and there is a Biblical reason why.

Excellence for the Christian leader doesn't begin with the work of our hands. While it arrives there, excellence begins with the posture of our hearts. Often how we relate to leadership and those in authority over us is a good litmus test for this.

Colossians 3 teaches Christians how they should interact in household relationships, not only between husbands and wives and parents and children, but also between bondservants and their masters. Colossians 3:22-24 says:

> *Bondservants, obey in everything those who are your earthly masters, not by way of eye-service, as people-pleasers, but with sincerity of heart, fearing the Lord. Whatever you do, work heartily, as for the Lord and not for men, knowing that from the Lord you will receive the inheritance as your reward. You are serving the Lord Christ.*

While we don't have bondservants and masters in 21st century America, we do have employees and employers, staff members and supervisors, as well as teams and their leaders. Christian leaders must be excellent in how they relate to those in leadership over them. Why? Because of Who ultimately leads us: Jesus Christ. Thus, our purpose in pursuing excellence is not just to get our supervisor "off our back" nor is it to earn favoritism. We ought to pursue excellence with sincere, humble hearts that recognize that there is a correlation between our respect for our earthly boss' authority and Jesus Christ's authority.

In addition, leadership is work, and our excellence in our work matters to God. We ought not to work well for the sake of impressing others. Rather, Colossians 3 implores us to work heartily, or *with the affections of our soul*, as though we're directly working for our Lord Jesus.

## The Fab Five Of Excellence

To this day, the 1991 University of Michigan basketball recruiting class is considered one of the most talented recruiting classes in the history of college basketball. Known as "The Fab Five," this team was not only fun to watch, but they were also very good. In fact, they were the first team in the history of the NCAA to make it to the National Championship Game with all freshman starters.

If I were to put together a "starting five" of the ways that Christian leaders should be excellent, the following list would be it. I call these *The Fab Five of Excellence*.

## 1. Effort

Leadership is work, and hard work is a necessary reality of this life. Ever since Adam and Eve ate the forbidden fruit in the Garden of Eden, it has been prescribed by God that we gain the necessary resources for life (food, shelter, clothes, etc.) through the toil of our labor (Genesis 3:17). But even our toil is dripping with the grace of God. He provides us with the resources, abilities, and opportunities to work. For those who are limited physically or mentally, God calls those who are able to work to invite them to join at the table of God's grace and provision through their work and generosity.

What is a natural response to God's provision of our resources, abilities, and opportunities? Worship. While we often think of music and singing as the means for worship, our excellent effort can and should be a means of worship as well. If someone were to offer you a distinguished leadership opportunity, isn't the principled response to honor his or her trust by giving our best effort? It follows that we should give our best, most excellent effort in the leadership opportunities God has given us.

## 2. Attitude

One of my favorite television shows is *Parks and Recreation*, a sitcom based on the zany happenings of the Parks and Recreation Department in a small, fictional town called Pawnee, Indiana. In the show a character by the name of April Ludgate is humorously depicted as the eye-rolling, disinterested, young intern whose every word is laced with sarcasm and who wittingly complains every time she is asked to do something. Her attitude makes for great comedy and banter—on television. In real life, a poor attitude rarely, if ever, is funny. An attitude of constant complaining, sarcasm, disinterest, or negativity drains those we rub shoulders with, including those trying to lead us. It can damage team chemistry, and regardless of how talented or zealous we might be, if we damage team chemistry enough we'll find ourselves no longer on that team.

The reality for leaders is that our attitude will rub off on those we lead. Leaders reproduce who they are, and the last thing we want to reproduce is a team of folks with a bad attitude.

May you and I always be reminded and aware of God's goodness and grace in the opportunities He gives us. An attitude of thankfulness and humility will help us not only be healthier leaders, but it will also help sustain us in the more difficult seasons of leadership when it's difficult to feel privileged for the role He has us in.

## 3. Time

Time is a vapor. It is here for a moment and then gone the next. And we have a limited amount of it, so we must be diligent with it. Obviously, we should not waste it with laziness or distraction. But we must also learn how to prioritize it. When it comes to prioritizing our time, there are two questions that we can consistently ask ourselves to help in our pursuit of excellence:

*Am I giving more time to that which is most valuable?* We should always allocate more time to efforts that are moving us toward the primary goals and targets of our leadership, even if those efforts are more laborious for us. I know that I have a natural tendency to want to give more of my time to tasks and efforts that I find to be more enjoyable or even easier. Can you relate? However, sometimes the things that are most important for us as leaders aren't always the easiest.

To be a diligent leader often means we have to be willing to sacrifice our comfort or ease for efforts that matter most in the long run.

*Do I set my schedule for what's next or what's best?* It's amazing how our task lists often fill up and multiply quickly. Part of being diligent with our time is learning to pause and asses our list of tasks and responsibilities. It is a common habit to prioritize what feels more immediate versus what is actually most important for the big picture of what we're trying to accomplish. Every week we should make it a habit to pause to prioritize those things which are most important and then plan as best as we can accordingly.

## 4. Quality

You and I are the workmanship of the most creative and excellent Artist in history. Who can match the beauty and quality of the work of His voice and His hand? God's work includes the beautiful kaleidoscope of humanity, the majestic sculptures of mountain ranges, and the awe-inspiring painting of the horizon at sunset. Nobody can match His excellence, but every one of us can reflect His excellence.

You and I were made in the image of this Creator, and we were made to reflect Him. As He is creative and skilled, so He has given us different gifts of creativity and unique skills. As the work of His voice and hands is excellent, may we strive for excellence in the work of our voice and hands. Even in the seemingly small tasks, producing excellent quality reflects the excellence of our Creator and brings Him glory. This is what it looks like to work with the affections of our soul.

## 5. Progress

A banner verse for encouraging young Christian leaders has always been 1 Timothy 4:12, which says, "Don't let anyone look down on you because you are young, but set an example for the believers in speech, in conduct, in love, in faith and in purity." When I hear this passage referred to, I often wish we would focus on the next few verses as much as we do on verse 12.

Following that famous verse, the apostle Paul goes on to encourage Timothy, a young pastor, to not neglect the ways God has gifted him. Even more, he implores him to practice his preaching and teaching of the Scriptures, and in verse 15, Paul tells Timothy: "Be diligent in these matters; give yourself wholly to them, so that everyone may see your **progress**."

What does this verse mean for us? Being excellent does not mean perfection. We are free from the pressure of being perfect because Jesus was perfect for us. However, we should be excellent in *pursuing progress*. God has gifted every leader with different, unique strengths and has placed us in roles with unique responsibilities. We can be excellent by growing in our leadership, our competency in our responsibilities, and by sharpening the skills God has given us. In doing this, God is glorified as others witness the ways that He is growing us.

If you're like me, sometimes you can become impatient in your progress. You desire to have more experience, aptitude, and maybe even weightier responsibility than you currently have.

As with many new leaders, there was once a time when the amount of zeal I had for voice in organizational decisions outmatched my level of experience. To put it frankly: I thought I knew more than I did or, at least, I wished I knew more than I did.

While serving on the staff team at one particular church, my zeal (and probably some of my impatience) was noticed by the pastor I served under. He encouraged me this great nugget of truth: "You know, Chris, it's okay to be where you are." And where I was at that point was that I had some, but limited, experience in my leadership role at the church. And you know what? That was absolutely okay—because that's where God had me. That was the season He was using to grow me.

Too often we can look too far ahead. With stars in our eyes, we look toward the next season and desire to be at a place in our growth and experience that we aren't ready for just yet. The danger in this is we can become so stir crazy for the next place, role, or season of leadership that we begin to be less present or faithful where God has us.

We need to guard ourselves against allowing ambition (even godly ambition) to convince us that we're ready for the next season of leadership when God clearly hasn't brought us there yet. When He brings you there, it will be as clear as the daylight and with the affirmation of leaders in your life. Until then, Christian leader, *it's okay to be where you are.*

While we are where we are, may we seek understanding, growth, and progress. We must be diligent and faithful where He has us. In doing so, God will already be preparing us for whatever season will come next in His perfect timing. Wherever God has you, be present and be excellent in your progress.

**The work of the Christian leader should be marked by excellence.** In His grace and kindness, God has given us opportunities to labor for Him. Our labor is an instrument for worship, so let us labor with excellence. Whatever God gives us, may we do the best we can with what we have—for Him. Along the way, let us honor those who lead us as we lead others. And may we labor, not to please or impress, but with the affections of our soul for Christ...

In our effort.

In our attitude.

Being diligent with our time.

Producing quality.

And pursuing progress.

Let us be excellent.

# Reflection & Discussion Questions

1. Which of the *Fab Five of Excellence* do you think comes most naturally to you? Which might present your greatest growth opportunity?

2. Read Colossians 3:22-24. How might we practice excellence in our relationship with a leader or supervisor when we don't see "eye-to-eye" with them?

3. What do you think it means to work *with the affections of your soul*? What might that look like?

4. Is there a way you might be more diligent and wise with your time as a leader?

# Coaching Moment

1. Ask your coach to share a best practice he or she has learned as it comes to relating excellently to a leader that he or she isn't in agreement with (especially when that leader is in a place of authority).

2. Share with your coach one skill or area of leadership you want to become more excellent in, as well as why you want to progress in that way. What might be a resource or potential opportunity that might help you develop in that area?

# CULTIVATING INFLUENCE

# 7

# ARE YOU TRUSTWORTHY?

You and I make decisions every day, both big and small, that are fueled by trust. Even the most seemingly simple actions can only happen because trust is in place.

Think of all the trust that goes into seeing our favorite band live in concert. We're willing to spend money on tickets because we trust that the band will show up ready to play well. We're trusting that the team of people setting up the sound and lighting equipment will be prepared, and we're trusting that all of the other people working the show will give enough effort for it to be an enjoyable experience.

But the trust doesn't end there. We show trust when we go online to submit our credit card information to a ticketing company to buy our tickets. We're also trusting that the company will be responsible with this important information and will only take the agreed-upon amount from our accounts.

Then we'll get in our vehicle and drive on roads and high-ways where traffic lanes are separated only by thin white or yellow lines because we have enough trust that the oncoming drivers are going to obey the same traffic laws that we do.

Without at least some level of trust, we would never do any of the things required to do something as simple as see-ing our favorite band in concert. In Christian leadership, as with so much in life, trust is the common denominator in the ability to move forward.

## Leadership Starts With Trust

As stated earlier, leadership is meeting people where they are, cultivating the right to point them where they should go, and helping them to get there.

But you and I will never be able to lead anyone anywhere without **trust**. It is a leadership "must-have" that builds influence. This influence then gives us permission to create movement toward the appropriate direction. Without trust, our team and organization will either go nowhere or we'll slog painfully along like a stalled car being pushed uphill.

Note the illustration. I call this *The Leadership Wheel*. Just as a vehicle needs wheels to move forward, these leadership "must-haves" work together to move a team and organization forward.

### The Leadership Wheel

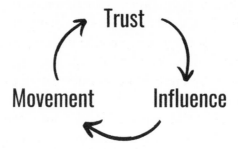

Let's define the three parts of *The Leadership Wheel*.

**Trust** is the assurance that people can rely on our integrity and ability. When leaders have the trust of their team they can begin to cultivate influence.

**Influence** is the permission to catalyze others. While influence can often come from organizational authority, the more compelling influence comes from healthy, organizational relationship. It is here the leader can give clear direction to team members to contribute toward the targets of the team and organization. *We will define and cover targets later in this book.*

**Movement** is realized change towards the target. When the team experiences that their efforts are adding value, then more trust is developed. The more trust is developed, the more influence the leader has, which provides more opportunity for the team to be catalyzed and move – and on and on the leadership wheel spins forward.

There is much that goes into making the leadership wheel spin, and we will unpack much of that, especially in regard to cultivating healthy influence, over the coming chapters. But first we must focus on trust. Without it, there is no influence and no movement, and we will not lead anyone anywhere.

## Common Questions

There are common questions we ask ourselves when we first begin getting to know someone, especially if the person holds a leadership role that impacts us in some way. Whether we lead them or they lead us, we often begin asking ourselves questions, such as:

- What is this person like?

- Where are they from?

- What are their interests?

- Do we have anything in common?

- What's important to them?

- What makes them tick?

- What is their posture towards me?

- Can I get along well with this person?

When we are in a leadership role, all of these questions are important, but they all circle back to one question that people want to know about their leaders: *"Are they trustworthy?"* If people are going to follow us, they want to know that they can trust us. And if the answer to this question is, "Yes" then already a significant step has been taken in that leadership relationship.

It is my experience that most people can live with differences between themselves and a leader, as long as that leader has their trust. What this really means is they don't need to have everything in common with a leader. They don't even need to necessarily agree on everything. But they must be able to trust this leader.

I've served and led on ministry staffs in a number of different contexts. I've served in the heart of the city. I've served in the suburbs. I've even served in a little town in west Texas – a vastly different community than where I grew up (in northeast Ohio). The times where I have been able to serve and lead people well who are different than me is when I've taken the time to build a foundation of trust. How does that happen? A foundation of trust is built when people believe they can rely on the leader's integrity and ability.

## Integrity

I recently had a conversation with a well-respected business leader who is also a leader in his church. Knowing that he's been part of processes for hiring people both in the market-place and in the church, I asked him what he looks for when considering hiring someone. Here's what he said:

> "I look for character, first and foremost. And when I say character, I mean I'm looking for integrity and humility. Integrity is critical. Without it, nothing works."

He's right. If people do not have the assurance that they can rely on us to have integrity in leadership, then we won't have their trust. This is not only true for those we hope to lead, but also for those who would lead us.

Of course, we want those who lead us to believe we have the smarts and skills to do well in our role, but just as important, if not more so, is the question, "Can they rely on us?"

Can they rely on us…

- To show up when we need to show up?

- To do what we said we would do?

- To be a team player?

- To put personal preference or convenience aside for the betterment of others?

- To be the same person every day, rather than be up-and-down in our temperament?

- To be wise with not only what we say but how we say it?

- To be honest, even if it doesn't exactly make us "look good"?

- To have integrity when they're not around?

My friend is correct when he says, "Without integrity, nothing works" for the Christian leader.

# Ability

People need to trust that we can do the job well. Whenever we step into a role, whether a volunteer position or hired one, there are always basic competency skills and experience required for the job. The people who lead us, as well as the people we lead, need to know we possess the basic competencies to fulfill our role faithfully.

At the same time, rarely does anyone step into a role with every skill, tool, or experience necessary for that role. There are two implications in this for us:

1. *We are free from having to act like we know everything and have done it all before*

As Christian leaders we should absolutely walk in confidence. We know who we are in Christ and we know that He continues to grow and transform us. At the same time, we need to guard ourselves from "putting up a front" and pretending we are further along than we are in our development.

I have never recruited or hired anyone (or seen anybody else recruit or hire someone) with the expectation that the person knows everything for the position. In fact, someone who thinks there is nothing to learn possesses a posture that would concern me. Rather I often have more trust in the person who has enough self-awareness to realize there is so much more to learn and develop, and they do something about it.

2. *We must take ownership of our "ability development"*

In asking some ministry and business leaders what they look for when hiring, I've noticed a trend. The well-respected business leader I mentioned earlier told me, "I'm looking for someone curious." An executive director for a well-known Christian company told me, "I always ask, 'What have you read?' Because I want to know that they are learners."

Again, rarely does anyone step into a role with every skill, tool, or experience necessary for that position. Therefore, Christian leaders must take ownership of their "ability development." Regardless of whether it's a volunteer or hired role, we must be learners. We must read, listen, and work to grow in our understanding. We must work to develop whatever core skills are required to do our jobs.

At a certain point, I realized I needed to grow in my communication and teaching skills. My supervisor at the time recommended a book on teaching well. Not only did I read it, but I also did the work to implement some of its helpful practices, even if it meant the painful shift of doing some things differently than I had before. Taking ownership of developing knowledge and skills takes work. People, especially coaches, will help point us in the right direction, but we have to put in the work, time, practice, and sometimes even our own resources. It's an investment. As we grow in our ability and show that we can do the job, we will build trust with those who lead us and those whom we lead ourselves.

## The Porcelain Goose

Sitting in the living room corner in the home I grew up sat a porcelain goose. It matched the rest of our living area's theme of an old, country home. My mother loved that beautiful yet fragile goose. But it was not the only fragile item in our home.

I must confess that in my days of being a young boy I broke my share of items in my parents' home: light fixtures, a window, and I completely shattered a storm door with a baseball—WHOOPS! However, I was wise enough to not let anything happen to that little porcelain goose my mother loved. If anything happened to that goose...well, *my* goose would have been cooked! That goose served as a beacon of caution, care, and warning to me.

Friends, trust is the Christian leader's *porcelain goose.* It is fragile. Let it serve as a beacon of caution and warning for us. May we exercise care as we lead with integrity. May we grow in the competencies and skills that we need to be better, faithful, and effective to the people to whom we're responsible. If we can do this, then we've accomplished the first step in leading others forward.

## Reflection & Discussion Questions

1. What are practical ways to build trust with others? How can you build trust with those who lead you? How can you build trust with those whom you lead?

2. What is a basic skill or competency that is necessary for your role? What is one way you want to better develop that skill or competency?

3. How can a lack of integrity break trust? How can a lack of ability break trust?

## Coaching Moment

1. Ask your coach to share a practical tip or habit as it comes to building trust with others.

2. Has there ever been a situation in which you have broken trust with someone, albeit unintentionally? Share about that situation with your coach. Ask him or her to help you process through what you could have done differently, as well as what you can learn and apply from that situation moving forward.

# 8

# RUBBING SHOULDERS

At 25-years-old, Dan was given the opportunity to pastor a church. This church, a mostly older congregation, was located in Amish country, Ohio. If you ever want to step back in time and experience life in the Midwest as it was a couple hundred years ago, visit Amish country. It's a beautiful area that is still very much rooted in its old Amish and Mennonite traditions.

So here comes the new, young pastor Dan: a 25-year-old, 6'4" tall, African American man to lead this older church congregation in Amish country.

As he stepped into this role Dan began to take note of who the real leaders, the real *influencers*, were in the congregation. As Dan puts it, "This is one of those churches that you're the leader if you've been around longer than anybody else." And who was that person? It was a 79-year-old, short, white woman named Mattie.

Dan and Mattie were two very different people. Outside of their faith in Christ, they had little in common. And I don't know about you, but I don't know many folks in their seventies who are excited about being led by someone in their mid-twenties. But Dan knew that if he was going to lead that church, he had to lead the leaders—starting with Mattie.

Dan learned that Mattie loved to cook and was actually able to invite himself over to her house for breakfast. That initial visit turned into a weekly occurrence in which Dan would show up to Mattie's home. Before heading out, Dan's wife would sometimes joke with him, "Are you going to see your girlfriend today?" And he would respond with a smile, "Yep!"

As Dan tells it, "I'd go to her house, sit down, and we'd talk. We wouldn't talk about church stuff. We'd talk about life, so I could get to know her as a person. I did that week after week after week. After a while she started to open up."

In their conversations Dan learned that Mattie, being older, often felt lonely and struggled to connect with people. He also learned that she was saddened by the fact that she hadn't held a baby in years and missed the joy of holding a little one. She wanted to serve in the church's nursery, but it was impossible for her to do so because of her age and health.

The next week, per usual, Dan woke up early to head to Mattie's house for breakfast. Only this time, he brought a guest with him—his three-month-old baby daughter. As he walked into her kitchen that morning, he asked, "Mattie, could you hold my daughter?" As she held Dan's baby girl, Mattie's eye became blurry with tears of joy. Dan always says about that moment, "From that point on, we were friends."[1]

## Presence

Dan cultivated influence with Mattie because he was willing to *be present* with Mattie. He not only made himself available, but he also was intentional to meet her where she was. Dan became a wiser and better leader because he took the time to *rub shoulders* with Mattie, understand some of her world, and learn how he could serve her well. And make no mistake; good leadership is always accompanied by a willingness to serve.

Dan was able to do all of this because he made the choice to be present.

## Servant Leaders Are Present

Presence is one of four factors (to be covered over the next four chapters) that helps leaders to cultivate influence. Leaders might cultivate influence for a host of reasons. For the Christian leader, our "why" for cultivating influence ought to be that we are **Servant Leaders** – we lead in order to serve and benefit others and because we model our leadership after how Jesus Christ led (which we'll look at in a moment).

**Presence** it is simply the act of intentionally making yourself available. If we want to serve and lead people well, then the first step is to be present with them. We need to meet with them where they are and make them aware that they are known and valued. We need to understand their world a bit in order to know how to serve them well. And we need them to understand some of who we are, what we are about, and why they can trust us as we make asks and give direction.

Being present does not mean that the Christian leader needs to have a significant relationship with everyone they lead. That's an impossible expectation. However, Christian leaders should have *some presence with all* and *more presence with some*. Jesus was a master at this.

## Jesus' Example

During His earthly ministry Jesus had thousands of people who came to hear Him teach, many of whom hoped that He would perform a miracle for them. In a way, Jesus had some presence with them. But as we look deeper into the Gospels, we see people who Jesus chose to intentionally have more presence with.

In Luke 10 we see Jesus sending out seventy-two of His followers. These were folks who Jesus had influenced and catalyzed to go and proclaim His message that the Kingdom of God had come near. For them to not only know His message but to also trust Him enough to follow His direction, Jesus would have had to spend time being present with them.

In addition, Jesus spent a greater amount of time being *present* with his twelve disciples. Mark 3 tells us that Jesus called and appointed "Twelve (disciples) so that He might *be with them* and send them out...." He needed to have greater influence with them, so He invested much time being present with them.

This was true even more so with three of those twelve disciples: Peter, James, and John. In fact, they are the only disciples mentioned to have been with Jesus during a couple key moments during His time on earth (His transfiguration on the high mountain and during His prayer in the Garden of Gethsemane). Now knowing the leadership roles that Peter, James, and John would have in the early church as well as their writing some of the New Testament, it's not a surprise that Jesus was so intentional to be with them.

As we've seen, during His earthly ministry Jesus had some presence with all, but He had more presence with some, specifically those He wanted to influence and catalyze for His mission.

## How To Be Present

What practical steps should the Christian leader take to be present in order to cultivate influence with others?

## 1. Be Available

Making ourselves available is a simple yet necessary posture for any leader. Being available is more of a posture and attitude we have towards others, rather than a skill.

In talking about how the best managers would be wise to make themselves available and approachable, the authors of *The Leadership Pipeline* put it this way:

> *People sense when the boss is approachable. Everything from his speech to his body language communicates accessibility (or the lack of it). This is really much more of a value and time-application issue than a skillset. When managers believe that being approachable is crucial to their leadership role, they make themselves available, both physically and emotionally.*[2]

Christian leaders need to be available as well as approachable. Still, the best availability needs to be disciplined. For instance, being available does not mean being willing to be interrupted or distracted with every phone call, email, or knock on the door we receive. If we're present but distracted, are we truly present? In other words, we should be approachable and be available, but we shouldn't feel guilty for having the discipline to ask somebody or something to wait until we can give them our full availability.

This kind of discipline is especially true for those of us who are in church ministry roles. There are definitely times of emergency where we need to quickly make ourselves available to people, so it's important for us to recognize and allow ourselves to be interruptible and present with our people in their hour of emergency.

At the same time, there are times when people will want to connect with us over a myriad of different questions and needs. I would suggest that ministry leaders have a plan for prime times when we are going to be most available. I also suggest deciding the times you are going to choose to be less available and to honor those times. This is especially pertinent for those of us who have family who need our availability. Our spouses deserve our presence. Our kids do as well. And our number one ministry is to our families.

## 2. Be Intentional

More than likely, there are already opportunities for you to rub shoulders with the people of your church, company, or organization. Be intentional to be present there. If you're in ministry, where are the natural places that your people show up?

On one ministry team I served on, myself and other leaders made it a point to be present at Friday night football games as much as we could because we knew that's where the students and families of our communities would be. It's here that I saw another example of the positive effect presence has. Because we had key influencers present there, over time we saw some of the football players from the local high school actually become an integral part of our church's student ministry. We also were able to partner with student leaders to launch a Fellowship of Christian Athletes huddle in one of our public high schools. God used our intentional presence to cultivate influence.

If you're in the marketplace, what are the natural times when people are together? I've read stories of upper-level executives making themselves available from time-to-time during the lunch hour to be present with staff. Their willingness to "rub shoulders" with staff made a positive impact on morale as well as on their ability to influence staff and move their organization forward—all because these executives made it a point to be present.

## Don't Underestimate These

Sometimes leaders have to initiate and develop opportunities to be present. As we do, we should not underestimate the impact that shared experiences, laughter, and food can have on the ability to cultivate influence.

A friend once told me, "Don't ever underestimate the power of getting away together." He would know too. He'd worked for years with an organization that trained and mobilized young leaders. There is something about shared experiences that builds relationship, bonds, and influence.

Leaders should often provide opportunities for people to laugh together as well. Believe it or not, laughter plays a significant role in influence. We have scientific research that tell us that laughter contagiously forms social bonds.[3]

Finally, in His goodness God has provided the common grace of taste. Whether we're a Christian or not, God has given us the ability to taste and enjoy good food. *Can I get an amen?!* But Christians should probably be *pros* at enjoying food because eating together is such an integral part of our history. In the early church, while participating in their mission of making disciples, early Christians got together to enjoy meals often. Acts 2:46 tells us, "They received their food with glad and generous hearts." So, whether you're leading in a church, non-profit, or for-profit organization, invite others to participate in this common grace and be present with them.

**Christian leader, be present.** Be intentional to make yourself available. Meet people where they are and make them aware that they are known and valued. As it comes to your role, have some presence with all but have more presence with some. Be approachable. Look for opportunities to rub shoulders and have shared experiences. And as you're present, you'll cultivate influence to both serve and lead others well.

# Reflection & Discussion Questions

1. Where are there natural opportunities to be present with those whom you lead?

2. What does it look like for a leader to be approachable?

3. How can distraction undermine our ability to truly be present?

4. What are practical ways to be disciplined as it comes to availability? How can a lack of discipline in this area have a negative effect on a leader or those they lead?

# Coaching Moment

1. Ask your coach to share how he or she navigates being present, approachable, and available to others while also remaining disciplined with his or her time and attention.

2. Share with your coach what opportunities are already available for you to be present with the people whom you lead. If options seem limited, what is an idea you could initiate in order to be more present?

# 9

# TAKE IT TO THE BANK

During the 18th century a small, yet significant product was created that would change the banking world forever. It used to be that if people wanted a record of all of the deposits and withdrawals made to and from their bank accounts, they would have to physically visit the bank and ask a banker to see their account records.[1] The bankers would then bring out huge, leather-bound ledgers that kept records of their customers' transactions. As you can surmise, only the bank (not the customer) had a complete, official record of the customer's deposits and withdrawals.

It used to be this way, until the creation of the *passbook*. About the size of a passport, this little booklet, owned by the account holder, allowed an individual to now keep a detailed record of every deposit and withdrawal in his or her bank account. For every transaction, people would take their passbook to the bank, where it would be passed between the account holder and the banker for updating.[2] With their passbook in hand, the account holders were now empowered to be wiser in managing the transactions on their accounts.

## Relational Investments

Relationship is required in order for leaders to have influence, and investment is required in order for relationships to be established and grown. Therefore, if we want to cultivate influence, then it will take **intentional, relational investments** over time. A lot of leaders call this building "relational equity."

Much like a bank account, every relationship has a history of deposits and withdrawals. **Deposits** are positive interactions and shared experiences between people. They add value, goodwill, and trust.

**Withdrawals**, on the other hand, are interactions that cost one or both parties something. They are the red on the ledger, if you will. However, not every withdrawal is necessarily a negative interaction. Leading others well sometimes requires well-calculated withdrawals.

If you or I was going to manage a bank account well, we would be wise not to make more withdrawals than deposits. If we do, then the account will go into default. Similarly, relationships require wise awareness of the account balance. If enough positive, relational deposits are made over time, we will have influence. However, if people have enough negative interactions with us over time, typically that relationship will go into default.

The same can be true if we ask too much of people over time. Christian leaders are *servant leaders*, and we must be careful to avoid making too many relational withdrawals too quickly.

I've seen leaders, especially those who are new to a role, quickly burn through the small amount of influence they had because they made too many asks or too big of an ask without making enough investment themselves. When we do this, there is risk for making team members feel as though they are a means to our end rather than a co-investor with us.

## Transaction Trends

In interviews and conversations with established leaders of different churches, companies, and organizations, I've asked what trends they've seen when it comes to the interaction habits of newer or younger leaders in their organizations. This included both deposits and withdrawals.

I began to notice a similarity in their answers and key themes that are important for all of us to take note of as we think about our interpersonal habits as Christian leaders. Note that these interaction habits not only affect the influence with peers or those we lead, but they also affect the influence we have with those who lead us (supervisors, etc.).

## Deposits

### 1. Positive Interpersonal Skills

This may seem very fundamental, but the value of positive interpersonal skills was brought up time and time again in my conversations with established leaders. The consistent habits of making eye contact, having the ability to carry a conversation, and having a kind disposition are basic but necessary skills in making small, consistent deposits in the bank of relationships. Over time, these positive interactions really do build influence.

Another valuable interpersonal skill is the ability to listen well—this is especially true when we lead people older or more established than us. They want to know they are heard and that you value their experience and perspective.

## 2. **Humility**

Humility can play out in a number of different ways when it comes to interpersonal interactions. Here are a few questions that might help us gauge our level of humility:

- Do you seek truth, or do you seek debate?

- How do you handle situations in which you are wrong?

- Do you know your strengths, as well as where you need to improve?

- When given the freedom to try something new, do you still stay within the guidelines of your organization?

- Are you faithful in the small things?

As the last question points out, our humility plays out when we decide to give our very best effort to be faithful in the seemingly small things long before we are asked to take on weightier things. What's the importance of these seemingly small things? As Luke 16:10 tells us, "Whoever can be trusted with very little can also be trusted with much...."

I once heard a story of a young man who felt God was calling Him to vocational ministry and to teach the Scriptures, so he approached the lead pastor of his small church to share what he sensed God was calling him to.

His pastor, having known him for some time, affirmed this young man's desire to be in ministry and to teach. Then his pastor said, "You want to teach? Great! Here is your first ministry assignment." He then proceeded to hand the young man a vacuum and asked him to sweep the floors of the church for the next three months. During that time, the young man gave his best effort every week to make sure the carpets were spotless before and after every Sunday service.

After those three months, the young man again shared with his pastor how he felt led towards ministry and teaching.

His pastor again affirmed his desire, endorsed the excellent work he did sweeping the church floors, and said to him, "Great! Here is your next ministry assignment." He then asked the young man to set up eight to ten chairs in a circle and told him that for the next six months he was going to lead and teach a small group of elementary-aged boys. And so, each week over the next six months, the young man showed up early, set up the chairs, and was prepared to lead this small group of boys well.

When the six months were almost up, the pastor approached the young man and said, "Would you be interested in having a conversation about teaching?"

As that story reveals, humility and patience are necessary to be diligent in the seemingly small things over time. But every time we are faithful with the little things, we make deposits that cultivate influence, and we are seen as trustworthy enough to be given that which is weightier.

*Before I move to the next point I want to pause and recognize something important and wonderful. Some reading this may be in a similar circumstance to the young man mentioned as you may be wondering if God is calling you to pastoral ministry.*

*While God invites all of His people to be part of His work of extending His Kingdom, the Scriptures are clear that He calls some to very particular roles of leadership in order to serve and equip His church (Ephesians 4:11-13).*

*If you have felt "the tug" of God moving you to explore this potential call I want to encourage you to do that. The next, best steps I would recommend taking would be: to pray constantly and ask God to give you clear discernment, to meet with a pastor whom you trust and who has already navigated the call to ministry, and to utilize a good resource to help you process what this calling might look like.[3]*

## 3. Team Player

In a conversation with a company's vice president, the VP shared how valuable "flexibility" is to him. As he put it, "I can't give someone responsibility if I don't think they have flexibility. I need an *X-factor*, who is up for doing anything."

Flexibility is necessary for being a team player. "Team players" are willing to be open-handed with their personal conveniences, benefits, and perspectives for the greater good of the organization. This VP shared that a problematic trend with some of his employees has been their unwillingness to step out of their "wheel-house" (the things they are most experienced in and comfortable with) and step up to contribute in other areas where there is need.

This should not be a habit of the Christian leader. If we are going to be servant-leaders then we must be team players. When we "make plays" to help the team win, it makes a significant deposit in the bank of relationship with our teammates, as well as those who lead us.

An old friend of mine shared a story about how he ended up cultivating influence with his leaders—simply by moving some tables. He was an associate pastor at a church that shared a facility with a school. Typically, the cafeteria tables from the school were stored in a room on the weekends so they would be out of the way for Sunday's services and programs.

One particular week, the floors had been cleaned and the tables could not be stored where they typically would. As a result, these cafeteria tables somehow ended up being propped up in the church lobby. My friend noticed that this would not only be problematic for traffic flow on Sunday, but it would also lessen the excellence of the lobby area's presentation for guests.

Even though these tables were not within his specific area of responsibility, he took initiative, found a different spot for the tables, and asked a couple other staff members to help him move the tables there. During those thirty minutes of work, my friend took initiative by his own volition and showed that he cared about the organization as a whole and not just his primary area of responsibility. That is being a team-player.

Now that we've looked at a few examples of deposits, let's look at a few common withdrawals.

# Withdrawals

### 1. Poor Interpersonal Skills

Consistent, poor interpersonal skills can have a negative impact on our ability to cultivate relationships with others. A lack of wisdom with what we say and the tone in which we speak to others can make significant withdrawals.

One established leader shared with me a time when she received feedback from a co-worker who told her that her directness was "like a knife." As a result of this experience, she shared with me: "I've learned one of the best questions we should all ask from someone we trust is, 'How do I come off in meetings and conversations?' Then we need to take the time to listen, without defending ourselves, say 'Thank you,' and go do something with that feedback."

### 2. Unrealistic Expectations

Influence must be cultivated by making investments over time. One of the consistent themes I hear from established leaders who make hires of new or young leaders is that the new leaders' expectations for influence in their organizations don't match their level of investment.

Leaders who are younger or newer often bring great passion, zeal, and fresh thinking. But when this zeal is matched with a lack of patience, the opportunity for frustration can arise—both for them and for established leaders who have been around longer than they have.

Some established leaders have told me that they often experience newer staff who expect to be part of the organization's discussions or decisions, but this desire just doesn't match their level of investment or experience. One business leader shared with me, "Sometimes we have employees who expect to be involved to the point where it's as though they have ownership stake in the company. I want to see that passion, but that isn't something you can have right away. It is something that is earned over time."

This can be frustrating for hard-working, passionate new leaders, especially if they walk into an established leadership situation. Because they don't have the influence yet, they don't see much movement in regard to their ideas (that they are very passionate about) being heard or implemented. This is a significant withdrawal for them. This can lead to being offended or "shutting down."

On the other side of the coin, there are people, often established leaders, who have greatly invested their hard work and dedication to help bring that team or organization to the place it is now. Sometimes when a new leader begins to ask questions or make suggestions it can feel as though this new person is disregarding and undermining their established experience or work, especially if those questions and suggestions aren't articulated well. This is a withdrawal for the established leader who has been investing over time.

One key to easing this tension is for new leaders to have **resiliency**. New leaders who are willing to be patient and invest over time are the ones who will overcome this. As a pastor friend of mine puts it, "They are able to bottle that passion up until they have gathered the influence." And when it is time for new leaders to ask questions and make suggestions, they must do it with humility and care.

## 3. Change

Any change is a withdrawal. The greater the change, the costlier the withdrawal. Why? Because change is almost always tethered to some kind of pain. Whether it be inconvenience, fear, or even the simple shifting of expectations, change creates pain for people. But change is a necessary pain that must be navigated well by the Christian leader.

It is impossible to stand still and move forward at the same time; therefore, changes are necessary to move teams or organizations forward. As such, withdrawals are necessary.

Here is one key to easing the pain and cost of making or introducing almost any change: *Changes should be catalyzed by conversations, not by meetings.*

Before we recommend or institute a change in a meeting, we will "ease the pain" if we have a conversation (often multiple conversations) with the right person or people. This should happen before we're in a meeting with a larger group of people. Who are the right people? Typically, they are those who have the greatest investment, influence, and weight of responsibility in the scope of what the changes will affect.

Please be careful how you go about this. The point of having these conversations is for the sake of serving teammates well in the process of potential change. We ought to be careful not to use conversations to bypass or manipulate the process. Do that and you will forfeit significant, if not all, relational equity with other leaders.

While surprises are normative to the experience of being a leader, I've never met a leader who likes them much. Most people don't. If you want to double the cost of a change, surprise the wrong people with the change. Rather than surprising them, invite them into the conversation. Give them time to consider, ask questions, and recalibrate their expectations. In so doing, you'll mitigate the cost and the pain of the change.

## Keep It Balanced

Having a balanced *passbook* in the bank of relationships matters. To cultivate influence it takes consistent, relational investment over time. And that requires patience and resilience.

A relationally healthy leader is a servant leader. Be sure your posture as a servant-leader is clear in your interactions with others. Treat people well. Take the time to have conversations. Speak with care and with an intentional tone. And please take the time to listen.

Serve well and faithfully in the seemingly small things. Have humility as you are faithful, and, at the right time, you will find yourself being trusted with more. Be a team player. Show that you care about your teammates as well as the organization as a whole.

## Reflection & Discussion Questions

1. What kinds of interpersonal skills often leave a positive impression on you?

2. What negative interpersonal skills are typically a turn-off to you?

3. Is being a team player important to you? Why or why not?

4. What is one way you can make a relational deposit with somebody you serve or work with this week?

# Coaching Moment

1. Ask your coach to share an example situation where he or she had to be a "team player." Ask what he or she did, why, and what was learned from that situation.

2. Share with your coach how you typically feel and respond when you are asked to do something you don't like to do. This could also include being asked to do something that feels outside of your comfort zone. Why do you think you feel that way? What might be a healthy way to respond to those asks in the future?

# 10

# STEP INTO THEIR PAIN

When I was twenty years old, I participated in an internship as a student ministry leader at a small church near my college. During that time, I had the privilege to get to know the lead pastor and his family. They were fantastic people, so warm and welcoming to me. I also learned that the pastor had some significant health issues and, as a result, had to have open-heart surgery.

Being so young, I really didn't feel equipped when it came to serving this family well. I didn't know what to say or how to be helpful—all I could do was to show up. So, that's what I did. On the day of the lead pastor's surgery, I came to the hospital early to be with the family. Before surgery they invited me into the pre-op room. They asked me to pray, and, intimidated by the weighty circumstances, I fumbled through a prayer.

While the pastor was in surgery, other folks from the church arrived, including some members of the student ministry. One of the pastor's daughters was one of our students, and we invited her to come and have lunch with us. I figured a little food might help to get her mind off things.

Little did I know how much our willingness to show up and step into the pain of a difficult day would mean to that family. The following are excerpts from a letter the pastor's daughter wrote to me shortly thereafter:

*Chris, thanks so much for rescuing me from what would have been 26 straight hours at the hospital on the day of my dad's open-heart surgery. Whether you realized it or not, just that one hour away from there with all of you meant a lot.*

*You've played a big role in me growing stronger in Christ, and that's important. Good luck with everything you do. Wherever you end up – whether it be leading another group of wild, caffeine-addicted youth kids armed with duct tape, trying to explain your Bible theology stuff to someone, or just jamming on your guitar...*

*Always trust God. He's got awesome plans for you. Someone once told me that...*

Living in a fallen world marred by the effects of sin means that pain is *going* to be a reality of life. It's going to be a reality for us, and it's going to be a reality for the people whom we lead and serve.

There are so many different ways that pain enters the picture. Sometimes pain will be the result of circumstances that are outside of the individual's control: sickness, death, family tragedy, and so on. Sometimes pain will be a result of our own choices, such as making an unwise decision or simply taking on opportunities that painfully cause us to grow.

God often gives Christian leaders the unique privilege of being able to **step into someone's pain**. It may not often feel like a privilege, but it is. Whatever the reason for the pain, God gives His people the opportunity to reflect Jesus' compassion by simply showing up in the midst of others' pain. By showing up, we are following the example of Jesus Christ (the best servant leader ever!) who had a habit of entering into people's pain with them. For instance, He showed up:

- When a woman, whose life was full of heartache, was fetching water at a well

- When a loved one, Lazarus, died and his friends were mourning

- When nobody wanted anything to do with the leper

- When the storms were too much for his friends

- When humanity needed a Savior

How people invite us into their pain might be as simple as a co-worker confiding in you that his or her marriage is struggling. It might be someone from your small group who shares a personal battle with anxiety or depression. It might be the family that is scared because of their father's significant health concerns. This is being invited in.

So, when we are invited in, how should we respond?

## Five Important Habits

There are plenty of books and resources on the market that address the topics of care and grief, and I will never pretend to be an expert in those arenas. At the same time, I've been blessed with some great coaches who have helped me understand five important habits that will help us respond well when someone invites us into their pain.

## 1. Expect To Be Inconvenienced

Pain is neither a respecter of persons nor schedules. As leaders we need to be aware that the pain of someone we serve and lead will be an inconvenience for us. This is where the trait of flexibility comes into play. Making ourselves available for even the simplest conversations where people can express their struggle will help us to serve these folks well.

A friend of mine recently shared how he has intentionally worked to build relationships with the people he leads. Being a regional vice president, he has a significant number of people on his team. Yet, because of his intentionality, God has given Him opportunity. A number of these folks have approached him to have a candid conversation about something personal happening to them or their family. His availability in the midst of the busyness of work has given him an opportunity to reflect the compassion of Christ in his leadership.

## 2. Don't Be Shocked

It's an already difficult enough task for many to be transparent and reveal their struggles and pain to another person. The only thing that makes it worse is if we respond with shock or surprise. Responding in this way can often unintentionally embarrass or humiliate an individual.

Transparency has always been a difficult thing for me. Frankly a lot of people, especially church people, have only added to the insecurity. I remember once participating in a small group where each person began to share some deeply personal experiences and past hurts. At a certain point, I had mustered up the courage to share a fear that had been cultivated out of some painful experiences in the church. Another group member's eyes opened wide as the person responded, "I can't believe that! That is absolutely heartbreaking that you

feel that way!" In embarrassment, I immediately began looking around the room for a dark hole to crawl into.

When people are transparent enough to share their pain
with you, the response in your eyes will often tell them all
they need to know about whether you're a safe person to
share life's hurts with. Keep your eyes kind, calm, and steady.
Listen well and understand that less is more as it comes to
responding with words.

### 3. Don't Try To Fix The Pain

When we step into someone's pain, we often desire to
offer the right word of encouragement or even a Gospel truth
that somehow eases all of the pain. While this is a commend-
able desire, it is almost always an unrealistic one.

Proverbs 25:20 tells us, "Whoever sings songs to a heavy
heart is like one who takes off a garment on a cold day, and
like vinegar on soda." In other words, sometimes we only add
to the hurt if we attempt to disregard the pain by forcing a
"positive spin" on someone who is hurting deeply.

More often than not, our best course of action is just to
be present, sit with them, and listen. If we do speak, it is often
best to ask questions. Why? Because asking questions might
help them process their pain and help you understand their
pain better, as well as give you more understanding on how
you might help them. Trying to help without taking the time
to listen often results in our operating out of assumptions.
And I've learned the hard way that operating out of assumptions does make a donkey out of us.

### 4. Know Your Limits

One of the best ways to help people well is to know when
you can't help them anymore. We should each know our limits when it comes to our expertise, availability, and resources.

In regard to my level of training, I recognize I am currently equipped to help somebody from a place of foundational, pastoral counseling. I can encourage people by helping them to understand what God says in His Word and how to apply it to everyday life.

I do not, at the time of this writing, have training to help people navigate issues such as trauma, anxiety, depression, addiction and so on. I know my limits. Therefore, when a conversation with someone bumps up against the limits of my equipping, I will be honest with them about that. Then I'll help them take the next step by connecting them with someone who is better equipped to help them in that arena. If available, I always make it a point to refer to someone who helps from a biblical worldview.

We also must recognize our limits when it comes to our resources and availability. Mercy should be a habit of the Christian life, but a lack of wisdom in our mercy shouldn't be. Christian leaders must be careful to know their capacities, including emotional and financial, and their time limitations. It is my view that it's never healthy for an individual to shoulder the responsibility of becoming "everything" for someone in pain.

## 5. **Pray On Their Behalf**

In the midst of our pain, God is always at work. In my personal moments and seasons of pain, I've found great comfort in David's words in Psalm 34:18: "The Lord is near to the brokenhearted and saves the crushed in spirit." For those in pain, God is not too far off. May we pray and seek Him on their behalf, whether or not they have been reconciled to God through Christ yet. May we pray for that! And may we seek comfort for them from the Great Comforter, who knows the innermost part of their heart and mind and loves all the same.

## When We Have Pain

When my wife and I had been married for about eighteen months much of our pain had come to a head. We'd been struggling for some time, and the combination of my fear of the future coupled with wounding from her past had driven a wedge in our marriage. There was a tapestry of tears, anger, unkind words, and, at times, an excruciating silence that loomed ominously over our relationship.

But I thank God we were not alone in our pain. We had dear friends and leaders in our life who were willing to step into our pain with us. They didn't neglect or reject us—they were with us. They prayed with us, stepped into gaps for us, and connected us to the help we needed. As I reflect on these friends now, my heart fills with gratitude for them. I have no doubt that their willingness to step into our pain was not an easy or convenient task for them. Yet, they were willing to do it anyway, and God used them to help change the trajectory of what was a very difficult season in our marriage.

When I think of our story, I know there are other stories of pain like ours. Please let me encourage you, as one who has been guided through pain, as well as walked with others through theirs – don't neglect the blessing of inviting someone into your pain.

If you are a pastor or serve on staff in a church or ministry setting, I'd like to encourage you specifically. Please – do not be so caught up in the pressure and responsibility of tending to the sheep that you aren't willing to be tended to yourself. Galatians 6:2 tells us to "bear one another's burdens, and so fulfill the law of Christ." We are often willing to bear the burdens of others, but when have you allowed someone else to bear yours? In those seasons when pain arrives, invite a trusted Christian friend or leader to bear it with you.

# Show Up

It is a privilege when someone invites us into their pain. May we show up and enter into it with them, reflecting the compassion of Jesus Christ. He came and entered into our pain with us in order to redeem and restore us.

As we enter in, may we do so wisely and...

Expect to be inconvenienced.

Not be shocked.

Not try to fix the pain.

Know our limitations.

Pray on their behalf.

And when pain arrives in our own lives, may we invite a trusted Christian to show up and step into our pain with us.

## Reflection & Discussion Questions

1. In your own words, explain why it is a privilege when someone invites us into their pain?

2. Can you think of a time when a friend was present with you in the midst of a painful situation or season in your life? How did God use their presence in your life?

3. How can being willing to enter into someone's pain help cultivate influence?

# Coaching Moment

1. Ask your coach to share about a situation in which he or she came alongside and supported someone navigating a painful circumstance. Ask what he or she learned from that experience.

2. Share with your coach what support you feel like you can realistically offer to someone navigating pain as well as the limits of what you can offer. When you arrive to those limits, what are potential resources and help you might point people to?

# 11

# BE PREPARED

Some things make other things better. They just do.

Let's start with something small and simple, such as a piece toast. In itself, a plain piece of toasted bread isn't very exciting. But add the right spread—a little butter, your favorite jelly or jam, or (my personal favorite) peanut butter—and suddenly what was once plain, toasted bread is now much tastier.

Now let's think a little bigger. Everybody enjoys going to the beach, right? But have you ever been to the beach on a cloudy, cold day? It's kind of a bummer. However, when the sun comes out and warms the day, your visit to the beach suddenly gets a whole lot better! The sun's rays bring warmth, and we get to take advantage of the different benefits the beach might offer: swimming, playing volleyball, and so on.

As we can see, some things just make other things better. They just do.

And for Christian leaders, preparation is one thing that makes us better. It just does.

**Preparation** is simply making ourselves ready.

When we give the appropriate time, thoughtfulness, and work to make ourselves ready for the responsibilities we have before us, we create the capacity for ourselves to do well in serving and leading. There are a number of ways preparation helps us to do this.

# Make It Better

Let's utilize the example of having to lead a meeting or gathering. Whatever kind of leadership you're in, there are most likely times when you have to lead one of these meetings or gatherings, and, in such moments, preparation helps us to be better leaders. Here are a few ways preparation makes us better.

### 1. Preparation provides occasion for excellence

Taking the time to prepare provides a higher likelihood that the task at hand will be excellent.

Typically, gatherings that are thrown together last minute are not as excellent as they could have been. Taking the time to prepare will help us to:

- Be more organized

- Better steward the time

- Have what we need in place to actually accomplish the task at hand

### 2. Preparation gives opportunity to define priority

In working with others, there are a million and one things we might want to discuss and accomplish. However, it is often impossible to discuss and do everything as quickly as we would hope. We must prioritize the things that are a priority.

Preparing well helps us to create priorities and guardrails for the things that matter most in our meetings and gatherings. Personally, when I'm leading a meeting that I know will involve much discussion and collaboration, I like to prepare a meeting agenda that outlines the priority items and how long they will be discussed.[1]

### 3. Preparation conveys value

Preparing well helps convey to others that we value them and their time.

Imagine if you were invited by a chef to come and have dinner at her new restaurant. She invites you to come at a certain time on a particular day. Now imagine if you showed up on the correct day at the proper time, and they weren't prepared for you to be there. There was no one to greet and seat you. There were no clean dishes or flatware, no menus available, and they hadn't readied the kitchen to prepare your food. Would you feel like you and your time was valued? I doubt it.

Preparation conveys that we value others. And if we want others to value the time we are together—whether it's a small group time, team meeting, or church gathering—we must first show that we value the time by preparing well.

### 4. Preparation helps us communicate better

What and how we communicate matters. Taking the time to consider *what* we want to communicate to those we lead as well as *how* we want to communicate those things will help us to be better, more clear communicators.

*We'll talk more about communication in later chapters.*

## 5. Preparation creates margin for presence

Rare should be the time when we are "scrambling" before a meeting or a gathering time that we are leading. Preparing well helps us to create margin before the time so we can be present and "rub shoulders" with the people whom we lead. Being present and connecting relationally will help you engage those you lead during the time and vice versa.

Years ago, a ministry I led hosted a Christmas event for young people and encouraged them to invite their friends. We called it "The Christmas Extravaganza." The event boasted lots of food, over-the-top games, and a guest speaker.

We invited a local professional athlete to be the guest speaker. While he did not need to arrive until near the end of the event, he came early and participated in some of the over-the-top games *with* the event attendees. I still have pictures of high school students pushing this large, muscular, professional athlete on a scooter board around our obstacle course as they raced against another team.

When it was time for him to speak, he had the attention and engagement of every person there as he spoke. Why? He showed up early, prepared, and created margin to be present and rub shoulders with people before communicating.

## 6. Preparation helps us bring our best thinking to the table

Suppose instead of leading a meeting or gathering, we're invited to a meeting with the executive leadership in our organization. When we're "invited to the table," we need to be prepared to bring our best thinking, to communicate it well, and to invite our leaders into the conversation.

My friend Tom tells the story of when he was about twenty-five years old and working for a family book and video distributor. This was the mid 1990s, and the Internet was just becoming "a thing." Tom approached his supervisors with an idea that he thought might be successful: an online bookstore. His supervisors responded that the Internet was just a fad, so they didn't want to put the resources into something they didn't think would last.

Now, I don't have to tell you how successful online goods distributors have been (Amazon, etc.). And I definitely don't have to tell Tom who still, every now and then, reminds some of those folks he once worked with, including the owner of the company (his step-father, by the way) that they missed the boat on his online store idea.

But in sharing this story, Tom humbly admits that he didn't "sell" his idea well.

He didn't communicate the idea well nor did he do enough research to support it. He also admits that he didn't do a good job of communicating the idea in a way that invited the leaders into the conversation and provided a way for them to have ownership of its vision.

It's all well and good to believe *that* an idea will be valuable to our organization. But if we aren't prepared to communicate the *why* and *how*, then don't expect the idea to gain much movement.

### 7. Preparation pauses us to invite God in

This is truly the most valuable aspect of our preparation. If you're like me, leadership involves doing a lot with seemingly not enough time. In all of our activity it can be all too easy to forget that the most valuable activity is God's. As we are doing our best to be faithful to serve and lead well, may we not forget that He is the true and ultimate source of wisdom, knowledge, and understanding.

Proverbs 2:6-8 tells us,

> *For the Lord gives wisdom; from his mouth come knowledge and understanding; he stores up sound wisdom for the upright;* he is a shield to those who walk in integrity, *guarding the paths of justice and watching over the way of his saints.*

If we truly believe that He is *the* source for wisdom, as Christian leaders may we pause to seek the all-knowing God. Whatever kind of leadership role we are in, may we approach His throne and humbly ask Him for the wisdom to lead and serve for His glory and His Kingdom's sake.

## We Can't Always Prepare

As leaders, we will not be prepared for everything we face. This is another reason why prayer is so vital. It is my view that in leadership (and in most areas of life) we are rarely aware of just how dependent we are on the grace and activity of God in every moment.

Part of God's grace and activity in our lives is that He provides resources that are available to us when we face new challenges. It is wise for every leader to develop a list of places and people we can glean from as we navigate the challenges of leadership.

As one pastor told me, when it comes to hiring and developing leaders, "I'm not looking for someone who has all the answers, but I am looking for someone who knows where to find the answers."

Please allow me to reiterate why having a coach is so valuable for every leader. A coach can help us navigate new challenges, and they might also know of resources and people that can help us when they can't.

## The Risk of Being Over-Prepared

Some of us are so organized and so good at preparing that we can *over-prepare*. This is a leadership weakness of my own. If over-preparation was an Olympic sport I would probably own a bunch of gold medals by now.

There is often a fine line between being prepared and over-prepared. If we "overdo it" in our effort to be prepared, there is risk for us to actually paralyze ourselves, our efforts, and the efforts of others.

An unintentional fallout of this is that we may come off as impersonal or uninterested in the contributions of others because we have mapped out every little detail ahead of an effort. Or we might actually mismanage our time because we have given too much of it to details that are not necessary to our primary responsibilities.

Some of us need to give ourselves a little grace and know that preparing well doesn't mean every detail of every effort plays out exactly as we think it should. Preparing well means that we've given the appropriate time, thoughtfulness, and work to ready ourselves to lead and serve well.

## Reflection & Discussion Questions

1. How often is prayer part of your preparation? In what way would you want to build habits of prayer into your times of preparation?

2. How can preparing well help us to cultivate influence in order to serve and lead others well? How might not preparing well undermine our ability to cultivate influence?

3. What is an example of a time or effort where you prepared well? What did you do to prepare well? What were the benefits of preparing well?

# Coaching Moment

1. Ask your coach to share any best practices he or she has learned as it comes to both the preparation and prioritization of tasks.

2. Share with your coach what your habits of preparation typically look like. What do you do well? Where you might you have opportunity to develop? Ask your coach if he or she would give you any recommendations based on what you share.

# 12

# THE LEADER & THE TEAM

The Christian life is full of paradoxes.

A just God who extends perfect mercy.

A King who came to serve and not be served.

Salvation offered by grace and not earned by works.

When I look at Jesus' ministry on earth and His leadership, it is also paradoxical.

Jesus was and is the Son of God who came to both take away the sins of the world and to establish God's Kingdom on earth. He's the long-awaited Messiah to whom all of redemptive history points. And yet throughout His earthly ministry, He does very little, if anything at all, to glorify or exalt Himself. Rather, He is concerned with why His Heavenly Father sent Him and where He would send His followers.

**Jesus is clearly *the* example when it comes to leadership,** so let's examine His ministry, focusing on Jesus as the

Ultimate Sender and also on His team of ordinary people who became the sent.

## The Sender

During His earthly ministry, Jesus prioritized bringing His Heavenly Father glory by saying and doing whatever His Heavenly Father asked Him to do. In John 6:38 He says, "For I have come down from heaven, not to do my own will but the will of him who sent me."

In John 14, Jesus tells His disciples that He and the Father are *one*, and everything He's done and said is ultimately the Father's activity. Jesus—the miracle-working, captivating teacher who had a following that continued to grow—doesn't possess a hint of pride. Instead, He attributes everything good He's done to His Heavenly Father.

Jesus modeled humility in that He was not interested in glory for Himself, but for the One who sent Him—His heavenly Father. Pastor and author Tim Keller says this about humility: "The essence of gospel-humility is not thinking more of myself or thinking less of myself; it is thinking of myself less."[1]

## The Sent

Jesus also prioritized equipping His followers (His team of disciples) to join Him in what the Heavenly Father had asked Him to do.

Throughout the Gospels, we see Jesus present with His disciples and intentionally equipping, teaching, and preparing them to go and extend the Kingdom that was being established. Thus, from the very moment He called His disciples (whether they were on the shore cleaning their fishing nets, at the tax collection table, or from wherever else He called them) Jesus had a plan to prepare them for when He left.

In telling His disciples that He would leave and go to the Father, Jesus revealed, "Truly, truly, I say to you, whoever believes in me will also do the works that I do; and **greater works than these** will he do...." Greater things?! Jesus—the Savior of the world who came and brought the Kingdom of God into time and space—is telling His disciples that people who believe in Him will do greater things? Is this a legitimate thing for Him to say?

Well, let's look at history.

## Greater Things

Jesus was most likely arrested, put on trial, and crucified in the year 33 AD.[2] At His arrest, much of the influence that He'd cultivated was gone and many of His followers abandoned Him. As we talked about in earlier chapters, Peter, one of the three disciples with whom Jesus was most present, denied that he even knew Jesus, his friend and leader, when Jesus was on trial. Judas, the disciple who betrayed Jesus, ended up killing himself.

When Jesus was arrested and killed, imagine what might have been going on in the hearts and minds of His followers. Their leader, the man they had given their lives to follow, was brutally tortured and killed. Imagine the fear that gripped their hearts and minds, even after He was dead.

But the mission was not over; it was just beginning. We know that on Easter morning there was nothing, not even death itself, that could stop God's activity and work.

When Jesus rose from the grave He gathered the remaining eleven disciples to Himself, and He had other followers too. In fact, we know that Jesus taught 120 disciples for well over a month after He was resurrected, as well as appearing to over 500 people (I Corinthians 5:16).[3] And He readied His followers—His team—to be sent.

When we think about mobilizing a global movement, a mission that is for *the entire world*, 120 disciples doesn't really seem like a lot of people.

Still, Jesus gave His disciples the mission.

He told them to continue the work of the Kingdom by making disciples.

Then He did what He said He would do: He left.

He left...so they could do greater things.

In his book, *Rise of Christianity*, Rodney Stark gives us a picture of the remarkable growth of the Christian church over its first few centuries. While it's impossible for us to have exact numbers, based on what historians tell us, it's very plausible that in 150 AD the number of disciples grew to about 40,000 Christians worldwide. If you're doing the math, that's a little less than 120 years after Jesus ascended into Heaven. That is incredible growth for the time. Remember, back then they didn't have television, social media campaigns, or YouTube videos to help start movements.

By the year 200 AD there where were about 218,000 Christians.

Only 50 years after that—are you ready for this—the global population of Christians rose to over 1.17 million![4] If we fast forward to 2017, Pew Research has projected that there are 2.3 billion Christians globally, the largest religious group in the world.[5]

If you're like me, you hear that number and think, "Wow. That's great, but there are five billion people left who need to know Jesus, His gift of salvation, and be invited into the Kingdom! There is still a lot of work to be done!" Yes, there is my friends.

Those whom Jesus mobilized and who believed in Him did, in fact, do greater things, to the point of reaching billions for the kingdom.

# Looking At His Example

Obviously, Jesus Christ is the greatest example of what it looks like to have far-reaching influence as a leader. But what were some of the things He did to have this kind of influence?

First, we have to recognize that the ultimate catalyst is the activity of God. His will, activity, and purposes cannot be stopped. And, on this side of eternity, you and I can only begin to scratch the surface of grasping how He moves and works in the hearts of people.

At the same time, when we look at Jesus' earthly example we can glean much from His leadership to help us work towards greater things and influence. Here are three ways Jesus led that stand out to me:

1. Jesus' objectives were clear.

2. He was not only a servant leader but also a sacrificial leader.

3. He chose to do more by mobilizing a team.

Let's dive into these a bit…

## 1. Jesus' primary objectives were to glorify His Heavenly Father and to establish and extend the Kingdom

This is another reminder of what our ultimate goals should be for the leadership role God has us in. This is not limited to a role in a church or ministry, but any kind of role where God has you serving from a place of leadership. Our "secular contexts" are just as much of a ministry context as anywhere else.

My friend Mary is an educator and administrator for a local, public school. In sharing some of her story as an educator and how God has continued to move her into different leadership roles, Mary senses God's activity in and through her vocation.

She shared with me that she has a clear understanding that *God* has placed her in her current leadership role not just to work for the school district, but for Him.

In this work, she intentionally builds relationships with the educators whom she leads. She looks for practical ways to serve them, even sacrificing some of her time to help where she knows it will benefit them. She's intentional to "plant seeds" of the Gospel and has even led a Bible study during teachers' lunch. As she puts it, "It's my *Kingdom* priority to build relationships with the people I lead. I know I'm on this team for a reason. And this is my ministry."

Mary clearly has the right objectives in view.

## 2. Jesus was not only a servant leader but also a sacrificial leader

Jesus Christ was and is worthy of every ounce of service that is offered to Him. Yet, He chose (for a time) to give up so much of what He had a right to because He came not only to serve but also to sacrifice.

- He gave up the comfort and glory of Heaven to come and be with human beings broken and damaged by sin.

- He gave up the daily worship and admiration of the heavenly hosts to be continually questioned and ridiculed by human critics.

- While all of creation was made by Him, through Him, and for Him (Colossians 1:16), He walked humbly *with* that creation and eventually walked humbly to a cross to give what He did not owe in order that His creation might be redeemed and restored.

Jesus not only served; he sacrificed. Following His model of leadership will require that we make sacrifices as well. In a sense, we must "think of ourselves less" in order to benefit those we serve and lead. Here are a few practical examples of sacrifices we can make for the benefit of our team:

- We can sacrifice our preferences or what makes us most comfortable when we know it will benefit those we serve and lead.

- We can take on the tasks that are a bit less fun (and a little more painful) in order to set our team up to do things that will be more meaningful and impactful for their role.

- When we receive acclaim or a "pat on the back," we can redirect the praise to the individual on our team who was responsible for the excellent work in order that he or she might be affirmed and encouraged.

Even the simplest sacrifices for the benefit of others can reflect Jesus' model of leadership.

### 3. Jesus chose to do more by mobilizing a team

Jesus chose to have a greater and more far-reaching influence through a team. The mission and the work were not all accomplished on His own. He clearly had a greater vision for His team than they had for themselves. With that vision in mind, He invited them to join Him in the mission and work.

In John 15:15, Jesus tells his disciples, "No longer do I call you servants, for the servant does not know what his master is doing; but I have called you friends, for all that I have heard from my Father I have made known to you." Jesus Christ chose to mobilize a team for what He was asked to do. In leading that team, He not only spent the time to be present and have influence with them, but he also equipped and empowered them to go and continue the work to the point where they did greater things—even without Him in physical form. In doing this, He had incredible, far-reaching influence.

If we are going to follow Jesus' example, we must come to grips with this incredible truth about leadership: *It is not about us.* It's about God's glory. And it's about those we serve and lead.

- It is about having a greater vision for them than they might have for themselves.

- It's about taking the time to equip and empower them to go, to do the work, and to do greater things, even if that means we're not necessary at some point.

- It's about recognizing that we are limited, fallible human beings. It's not that we think less of ourselves, but we recognize that we can experience the joy of doing greater things and having greater influence than we could alone.

Jesus was and is the perfect leader. There's nobody better. There's no one who's done more than He has for the world. And there's no one who has had more influence. And in His model of leadership, He chose to have a team.

# Reflection & Discussion Questions

1. What are common misunderstandings of what *humility* looks like. Consider Jesus' example, as well as Tim Keller's quote about humility.

2. What are practical sacrifices you might make that would benefit those whom you serve and lead?

3. Why might it be important for a leader to prioritize equipping and empowering individuals on their team? How can this help a leader have greater influence?

# Coaching Moment

1. Ask your coach to give an example of when he or she mobilized a person or a team to go and do something. Ask what he or she did, why, and if there was something learned from that situation.

2. Share with your coach how well you do in "making asks" of others. Share if you find it to be difficult or not. Why do you think that is? Is there an inward fear that keep you from making asks of others? Ask your coach for recommendations as to how to make asks of others well.

# CREATING MOVEMENT

# 13

# THE STEWARD

"**Y**ou shall not pass!!!"
If you've read the books or seen the movies, you will recognize that quote from J.R.R. Tolkien's *The Lord of the Rings*.[1] I must admit that until the release of the films directed by Peter Jackson I didn't know much about the incredible, fictional world of Middle-Earth filled with fascinating characters and creatures such as hobbits, elves, and dwarves. But once I watched the films, I was hooked.

One of the great triumphs of Tolkien's story is how unique all of these characters and creatures are. In many ways, the heroes of the story could not be more different, and yet the characters are brought together in one, ultimate effort to save Middle-Earth from the evil Lord Sauron and his allies. To do this, they must destroy him by destroying his magical, golden ring, which is where his true power lies.

In his story, Tolkien doesn't ignore or apologize for the uniqueness of these heroes; instead he draws attention to their idiosyncrasies and how they each contribute to the challenge before them.

A wise wizard with a staff,
a mysterious man with a sword,
a zealous elf with a bow,
a crusty dwarf with an axe,
a proud soldier from a capital city,
and four, brave little hobbits from the peaceful countryside become a team...or as they're called in the story: a fellowship.

Admittedly, they are somewhat of a funny sight to behold. While they are very different and distinct from one another, they are bound by a common vision: to see peace return to Middle-Earth so their different people groups will be safe again. And it will take courageous contributions from every member of this team in order for their vision to become reality.

## Teams

What is a team, anyway? I like to define a **team** as a group of individuals brought together for a common purpose. And if we are in a leadership role, we are most likely leading a team of some kind. We might lead a team of staff at our job, a team of volunteers at our church or organization, or a small group of some kind.

Whatever the context, these teams and groups can be built in a number of different ways. We might inherit people who were already part of the group when we stepped into lead. Others might have been invited, recruited, or hired by us or by somebody else on the team since we've been leading.

Whichever way our teams and groups are built, the fact of the matter is we're going to be leading and working with people who are very different from us and one another.

On a team, every person brings a uniqueness with them—their personality, experiences, motivations, gifts, and capacity. These are all important personal resources that need to be *stewarded* well, and one of our primary responsibilities as leaders is to help team members do just that.

Historically, a *steward* has been defined as someone who is tasked with managing resources that belong to someone else. The uniqueness of every individual and what they bring to the team don't belong to us. It belongs to them. However, we have the privilege of helping them discover, employ, and leverage what they bring to the table to contribute toward the common goals of the team.

Think back to *The Leadership Wheel*...

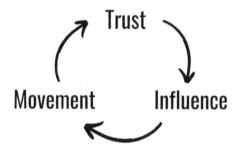

As we build trust and cultivate influence, we now look toward creating movement. *Movement is realized change towards the target* and the intended purposes for why the team and group are together. The reality of movement is that there will always be more when the collective is pushing than when the one is pushing.

Our role is not to do all the work of making the wheel move. Rather, we invite individuals on the team to contribute through their unique strengths, tools, and resources. It makes the team better. And it makes the wheel move more. Want to see more movement? Don't view the team as just a benefit—view it as a necessity.

So, for the betterment of the team, we will need to see ourselves as *stewards*, which leads us to confront a challenging tipping point of leadership.

## The Tipping Point

Call me optimistic, but I'm convinced most people want to do a good job in their designated role. Most of us feel the healthy tension of desiring to be excellent in what we're trusted with.

As one seasoned executive pastor put it, in our roles we all feel "accountable to our responsibilities." We feel accountable to doing a good job with the responsibilities that have been given to us. We want these things to be done well, according to the way we think is best.

When we step into leading, especially leading a team or group, there is a *tipping point* we will most likely feel. The truth of the matter is that we can't lead a team and do everything ourselves at the same time. If we try this, we will get buried beneath the responsibility. At some point, we need to be willing to be *tipped over* and allow team members to take on their portion of the responsibility.

Listen, I get it—there is joy in doing a good job.

However, there is a better joy to be embraced: It is the better joy of seeing someone on your team using what he or she brings to the table to do a good job.

So, a shift must begin to take place where we begin to *give* more, rather than *doing* more.

We give others opportunities.

We give them clear direction.

We even give them the appropriate bandwidth to make mistakes and learn.

But for those of us who are committed to excellence, this is a hard thing to do.

There is risk the task won't be accomplished.

There is fear that it won't go well or how we'd like it.

There is the uneasiness of not having control.

But, if we're willing to tip over just a bit and delegate some things, there is a better joy awaiting us as leaders.

I experienced this years ago as I was leading a ministry that God was growing. Early on in leading the ministry, much of what happened every week (specifically when we met on Wednesday nights) was dependent on my leadership and activity. This made a lot of sense at the time because the ministry and its leadership team were smaller.

Eventually, my leading this way did not make sense anymore. As our ministry grew, we ran out of gathering space, so we had to add a second gathering time, which meant doubling up the teaching, worship, and planned group activities. As our attendance grew, we not only needed more small groups for people to join, but we also needed to coach and develop more leaders to lead those groups!

I had to be *tipped over* so that others could take on important responsibilities. Here are some of the steps we took:

a. I stepped away from being a small group leader, so I could focus on being a coach for our small group leaders. In a way, they were my small group now. It was a little painful for me to do this because I loved leading my small group. I also asked a couple other experienced small group leaders to take ownership of coaching particular groups of our small group leaders. I made sure to be available to coach and support these coaches as well.

b. We delegated some of our weekly responsibilities to team members based on their giftedness, interests, and experience. I started giving worship leading opportunities to other people within the ministry. We handed off the technical side of worship to a team member who could not only lead it but also recruit and coach other people in the ministry to help him.

c. We "handed off" the weekly group engagement activities to our small group leaders. I asked a team member who had experience and gifting in leading these elements of our gathering time to come alongside and coach our small group leaders in the planning and leading of these activities.

d. Not only had I been leading and teaching on Wednesdays, but for a long time I had been leading and teaching another group on Sundays too. I knew we needed to recruit, equip, and empower a team of people to lead and teach that group...and that's just what we did.

When this *tipping over* began to happen, was it perfect? *No.*

Were there ways I could have coached people better? *Absolutely.*

Did people always lead efforts the way I would have led them? *Nope.*

Was it sometimes difficult for me to let go of control and ownership of some things? *Of course.*

But there is the beauty and greater joy of watching team members be equipped and empowered to do a great job together.

## Five Steps To Equip

There is a very simple, yet effective model I use for equipping a team member to do something that I have already learned to do. I call it the **Five Steps To Equip**. To better explain this model, let's imagine I were equipping and coaching you to lead a small group. This is the model I would use to equip you to lead a group:

1. **I Do / You Watch.** I'm going to show you what I do to prepare to lead a small group. Then you'll participate and watch me lead the group. Afterwards, we're going to debrief the group time. We'll discuss what I did when I led the meeting and why I did what I did.

2. **I Do / You Help.** In this step I'm still leading the group. However, now I'm going to have you help. I'll give you a couple responsibilities in both the preparation and leading aspects of the group time. Afterwards, we'll debrief together. We'll discuss what went well and what you might do differently next time.

3. **You Do / I Help.** Now you are the primary leader of both preparing for and leading the group. I'll offer help and coaching as you prepare. As you lead the group, I'll participate in the group time and be available to help you if necessary. After the group time, we'll debrief together what went well and what you might consider doing differently next time.

4. **You Do / I Watch.** This is similar to step 3, except that I'm not helping you prepare or lead the group time at all. The point of this step is for me to be assured that you are equipped enough to lead without my needing to be present. We will still meet after to debrief.

5. **I Leave / You Equip.** This is a key step that many leaders forget. I need to help you find somebody that you can begin taking through the "Five Steps To Equip." Sure, you may not have *tons* of experience leading a small group yet, but you can begin to share the things you have learned both from me and from your experience thus far.

*I purposely did not put a timeline on these steps. The amount of time at each step is going to be different for every individual being equipped. As the coach, you'll want to be clear as to what you're specifically asking the individual to do at each step. A lack of clarity will cause frustration, both for you and the person you are equipping.*

## The Ingredients Of A Team

Every team has its own *flavor*. On teams, members bring their own ingredients that contribute to the team as a whole, making that team unique. Just as Tolkien's collection of heroes brought together different and unique individuals that became a distinguishable collective, so are teams of people joined together. Here are some key ingredients that matter for team members and some insights on how to steward them well.

**Personality.** Everybody has a unique personality and temperament. The way we interact, speak, hear, communicate, and have our own natural inclinations are some of the things that make working with other people fascinating but also challenging.

While our differing personalities add lots of *flavor*, they can also bring an opportunity for misunderstanding and even miscommunication. Why? Because not everybody is like us. How we understand and perceive interactions will be different. I recommend having your team all take a personality test, such as the *Enneagram*[2] or *StrengthsFinder*,[3] and utilize those tools to discover how you can best relate to and communicate with one another.

**Gifts.** Take the time to learn what team members are good at and provide them opportunities to exercise and develop these gifts. When given responsibilities that match where people are gifted, team members will enjoy more. Of course, people have to do things in their role that might not be their favorite thing or in their natural skillset. We still have to do those things faithfully, excellently, and, hopefully, without complaint. But work with team members to think through and look for opportunities to do the things that match their gifting as well, and it will most likely energize them and increase their desire to joyfully contribute more.

The apostle Paul says of the church in I Corinthians 12, that "we are one body with many members" and we each have a role to play. In Romans 12, we see that every believer has different spiritual gifts "that differ according to the grace given to us, let us use them...." If your team is within the context of a church body, utilize a good spiritual gifts assessment test and help team members find the right opportunity to use those gifts for the body and the Kingdom![4]

**Experiences.** Every team member brings different life and work experiences with them to the table. Be intentional to hear, understand, and sympathize with peoples' personal experiences because often they'll see things that we cannot and have a vantage point on both life and work that we don't necessarily have. Giving an ear to hear, even if you can't necessarily empathize with their experience, will help us to be wiser and more intentional in our decision-making. Believe in what you have to offer, but believe in what others have to offer as well.

To be transparent, in my early days of leadership I would often become frustrated with people who did not see certain ideas or situations the way I saw them. And often these were folks who had more life and work experience than I did. Because I was so taken with the way I saw or felt, I missed out on having greater perspective and making better decisions. I didn't steward their experiences well and ended up undermining potential movement for the team and organization.

**Motivations.** Everybody is motivated in different ways and by different opportunities. Some people are motivated by challenges, while others are motivated by encouragement and affirmation. Other individual motivations might include working toward greater income, responsibilities, or influence. For some, especially in a volunteer role, a motivation might be the desire to have a positive impact for the greater good of others. Understanding what matters to people—their "why" if you will—helps us to motivate them to take next steps that will benefit both them and the team.

**Capacity.** This is the allocated time, ability, and energy that an individual is able to give. In speaking with a number of Christian leaders, both in the church and marketplace, it became evident to me just how important clear expectations and communication are in order for capacity to be stewarded well.

Clear job descriptions matter. Even in volunteer roles, individuals should have clear expectations as to what they are being asked to do.

A friend of mine, who served as an executive pastor for 35 years, shared that in working with church staff members he preferred job descriptions that included the percentage of time to be spent on each responsibility. I like this practice because it helps define not only the primary areas of responsibility, but it also gives clear expectations for how much time and energy should be allocated to the responsibilities.

He also often invited employees to work through what these percentages should look like, thus allowing them to have more ownership in their role. He and the staff member would then walk through what the staff member came up with, as he coached them to make it best suited for the role.[5]

This is a good reminder that, while it's important for every person to be a team player, our primary responsibilities must be prioritized first. If team members give too much of their time to something they enjoy doing but that isn't an organizational priority, then the organization as a whole suffers. This is why helping people to understand their primary responsibilities is important.

• • •

The truth of the matter is that **everyone wants to feel valuable to the team.** Give them opportunity to contribute in ways that makes sense for their uniqueness as they faithfully fulfill their primary responsibilities. Every leader faces the tipping point of being a steward, where we choose not only the joy of doing a good job but also the better joy of seeing someone else do a good job.

We may not be leading a group of wizards, elves, and hobbits, but we have the privilege of leading people who are uniquely made and wired. They bring with them a unique flavor: their personality, experiences, motivations, gifts, and capacity. As leaders we have the opportunity to help them steward these for the greater good of the team and organization.

## Reflection & Discussion Questions

1. What are some of the benefits of working with team members who have unique personalities, gifts, and experiences?

2. What are some of the potential challenges that come with a team of people who are uniquely different? How might we navigate these challenges well?

3. What is one unique gift or experience that you bring to your team?

# Coaching Moment

1. Ask your coach to share a time when he or she felt the "tipping point" of leadership. Ask what his or her initial, natural response was. Ask your coach to share any tips when it comes to delegating well.

2. Share with your coach an example of when you did something all by yourself when you probably should have asked for help. What do you think the motivation was for doing it yourself? What would you hope to do differently next time?

# 14

# CULTURE CREATOR

Today, we have access to many different kinds of music. In this digital age, we can listen to a seemingly unlimited range of genres, styles, artists, and playlists. The movement from records, tapes, and discs to the plethora of streaming services allows us to listen to an endless array of different songs, and listeners often can't help but be eclectic in their musical tastes. Ask any young person what they listen to. Sure, they might mention a preferred genre, but most will say, "I listen to a little bit of everything."

This was not always the case. There was once a time when the music we listened to might have said more about our life than the song we felt like streaming in the moment. Choosing a preferred genre was less like visiting the buffet at Golden Corral and more like deciding what neighborhood to live in. For many, becoming a fan of a genre or music group meant that we were connecting ourselves to a culture.

In the 1970s committed fans of the band The Grateful Dead were called "Deadheads." They not only listened to, but also followed the band to as many shows as they could. They even developed their own look, language, and community. At the very same time, the genre of Disco gave birth to a very different culture that featured bell-bottoms, big hair, smooth dance moves, and a *groovy* way of talking.

If I were to be part of a culture centered on a musical genre, I would belong with those who enjoy old, classic soul music. As my family knows, I'd rather listen to Sam Cooke and Al Green than anything currently on the Billboard Top 100. We could call ourselves the "Classics Crew." (I'm still working on the name, obviously.)

One of my favorite "classic" songs is "Man in the Mirror," performed by Michael Jackson. This song is loved for its message of self-reflection and the responsibility we have to care for our neighbors and communities. It is also very catchy and features a great hook that exclaims:

*"If you want to make the world a better place,*
*Take a look at yourself, and then make a change!"*[1]

The premise of this lyric is that if you want to see the world around you change and become more ideal, then that change has to start with you. This is true for all of us, especially leaders who desire to create culture. Want to see movement toward what you value? Take a look at yourself...

## Movement In Culture

It is people—their being, saying, and celebrating—that creates and contributes to the culture of an organization. Therefore, the people leading in the organization are **culture creators**.

As discussed in chapter 4, leaders are part of a community, and every community has a culture. Within this culture there is history, language, stated values, and implied values.

As leaders, we contribute to the creation and cultivation of each of these in the following ways:

- The way we lead and the decisions we make create history in the organization.

- The things we say and repeat consistently cultivate language.

- We often affirm or create stated values of our organization when we define organizational *targets* and *maps* (we'll explore these concepts in upcoming chapters).

- What we talk about and celebrate imply what we truly value.

In speaking with one executive pastor, he shared, "I've always believed 'culture creator' is a better definition of a leader. This is what leaders are trying to do—set culture." And what is the culture we are trying to create?

*The ideal version of culture is where there is integrity between the stated and implied values.*

The reality is that we would be hard pressed to find this perfectly idealized version of culture in any organization. If we set out to find one, we'll just find ourselves disappointed. That's the thing about creating culture: it's a never-ending work.

Frankly, it should be this way. The values of our organization should be so aspirational that it takes significant work over time to see them realized.

For many leaders, especially new leaders, this can often cause "rub." We can become frustrated because we believe in what the "ideal" culture is. However, we can feel tension because the ideal culture we, our team, or organization aspire to is not fully realized yet. Or we might feel our organization is not moving quickly enough to see it realized.

It is here that patience, resiliency, and taking responsibility for own leadership habits matter. We must be willing to put off our angst or impatience and commit ourselves to creating and contributing to the ideal culture within the space and scope of the leadership we're given. This is where we can begin to take first steps as culture creators.

## Where Culture Is Created

The popular sitcom *The Office* features the humorous antics of a paper supply company staff in Scranton, Pennsylvania. In one particular episode, the manager, Michael Scott, comes to realize that he is personally in financial trouble. One of the staff accountants, Oscar, helps Michael evaluate his income against his expenses. Oscar begins to realize many of the ridiculous and unnecessary credit card purchases Michael has made—including *multiple* deluxe magic sets. Who needs multiple magic sets?!

Another staff member, Creed, who is known for being somewhat of a sketchy con artist, recommends to Michael that declaring bankruptcy is the best option for a "fresh start." After thinking it through for a few moments, Michael walks out onto the middle of the office floor and exclaims at the top of his lungs, "I DECLARE BANKRUPTCYYYYYYYYY!!!"[2]

You and I both know that this isn't how declaring bankruptcy works. We don't just declare it by yelling it in the middle of a room and then, somehow, we have a financial reset to move forward.

The same is true when it comes to creating culture. We don't just declare it. We don't just make a statement, have one meeting, or make an organizational decision and somehow think that we're going to immediately move toward the ideal version of culture.

Rather, *culture is created in rhythms over time.*

## Our Being Before Our Doing

If leaders want to see a culture realized, then they must first be living that aspirational culture themselves. We can make all the grandiose statements about our culture we want. However, if we don't live the culture we want to see realized, then it does not make sense to expect that of the people we lead.

As leaders within an organization or on a team, we must not only be aware of the stated values, but we must be the first ones to live those out. For instance, if a company says it wants to be innovative, I want to know if its leaders are actually being innovative themselves. Innovation often brings risk, and I'll know if the company truly aspires to be innovative if the leadership is willing to assume the same risk of innovation themselves.

As leaders, if the things that we value fit the scope of the organization we're part of, how are we contributing to a culture that reflects those values?

Small group leader – Do you aspire for the people in your group to love their neighbors? Let me ask you: How are you loving your neighbors? What are the practical things you're doing to love your neighbors? And do the things that you're doing fit within your church's small group structure, values, and strategy?

## Two Things That Are Real

A few years ago, my family and I attended one of the family camps at Gull Lake Ministries Conference Center and Family Resort in Hickory Corners, Michigan.[3] Their team of college students and young adults are incredible in the consistent way they live out the stated value of Christ-like hospitality and their clearly implied value of enthusiasm! Seriously—they are *always* enthusiastic, even in the early morning. To me, that's very impressive. When I was a college student, I'm pretty sure I was still sleepwalking before 11am each day.

I reached out to their executive director, Daniel Wallace, to ask him what he has learned and applied when it comes to creating culture on a team. He shared two things that are *real* to him:

### 1. Culture is better caught than taught

Daniel shared that he makes it a point to be the first to do what he would expect his team to do. As someone who has seen Daniel and his team in action, I can tell you that the proof of this is, as they say, in the pudding. (What a weird saying, right?)

When we attended camp, it was clear who set the tone for the culture of hospitality and enthusiasm: Daniel and the team leaders. When we entered the first building on the very first day, Daniel was there to greet us with enthusiasm, stoop down and talk with our young kids, and show hospitality by offering help for how to make it a great week of camp.

Daniel shared two important questions that leaders should ask themselves: What do I want the culture to be? And am I doing what I want done?

### 2. What the leader does in moderation the team will do in excess

Because there are no perfect leaders, we all have leadership vices. These are growth opportunities in the "being" of leaders that can often work against the culture we are trying to create.

Just as it takes time for our character to be transformed, so it takes quite a long time for all of us to grow and mature as leaders. Over time, and if we are coachable, we will become aware of our own leadership vices. This awareness hopefully leads us to seek growth and development in these areas. *If *you need to, circle back to chapter Chapters 2 and 5, which cover being coachable and character.*

A common leadership vice can often be sarcasm. Yes, I know that sarcasm is a very normative part of our society. And it might even bother you that I called it a vice since most of us use it daily. But, as with so many things, just because something is seemingly normative doesn't mean that it isn't detrimental.

One of the things Daniel learned as a leader is that if he is just a little sarcastic then he should not be surprised if his team is very sarcastic. So, he made the decision to begin working towards not using sarcasm in his interactions with others. Instead, his desire was to let his "yes be yes" and his "no be no" (Matthew 5:37).

Now it's not as though, from this point on, Daniel was never sarcastic again. However, when he does "slip," he makes it a point to apologize and ask forgiveness from that team member.

As a leader, Daniel began to live it first. Then he was able to set the expectation for his team. He set the expectation that they were going to move toward their stated value of exalting Jesus Christ by moving away from sarcasm in their speech. In fact, he set out a "sarcasm jar" for the team. Whenever a team member used sarcasm, he or she had to put a quarter in the jar.

I'm going to be honest. If the summer camp I worked at as a college student would have done something like this, well, after a few days I would have been the one yelling, "I DECLARE BANKRUPTCY!!!"

Some team members did say to Daniel, "But sarcasm is my humor." Daniel kindly responded, "Well, it's going to change."

Over time the culture of the team moved away from sarcasm to the point where eventually everyone forgot about the jar. One day Daniel was cleaning out an office space and noticed the jar and the fact that it had not been used for quite some time.

He threw it away.

Culture had been created.

And it started with Daniel,

Because he chose to "be" the culture first.

## Culture Creation Through Regular Conversations

When my wife, Katie, and I were engaged to be married, I was pretty pumped. Okay, I was REALLY PUMPED. So much so that I talked about it all the time. I talked so often about how happy I was to marry Katie that I think my friends and co-workers, while they were genuinely happy for us, were a little tired of hearing about it.

It was revealed during our wedding ceremony by our pastor, who was also my boss at the time, that there had been a joke around the office in which staff would say to each other in jest, "Hey, did you hear that Chris and Katie are getting married?" If they would've had a quarter jar for sarcasm, I think it would've become pretty full rather quickly.

We all laughed, but our pastor commended us for the fact that we valued each other so much that we just *had* to talk about it. Jesus did say in Matthew 12:34, "Out of the overflow of the heart, the mouth speaks," right?

As culture creators, if we are truly committed to the values of our team and organization then we should be talking about them. We should be excited about them ourselves.

Leader, if you lead a local church body and a value of that church is to reach the lost with the Gospel (which it obviously should be, by the way), then we need to be the ones talking about reaching the lost. We should be excited and share our excitement when a lost person comes to faith.

Our values should be talked about with language that is consistent throughout our organization. I once served at a church in which the core values were *Worship, Community*, and *Mission*. Every "all-staff" meeting we would have team members share updates and stories. Every update and story was connected to one of three things: Worship, Community, and Mission. That was the language the team used. People didn't use other terms or phrases to describe these values. They used (say it with me) Worship, Community, and Mission.

## Celebration & Stories

Ready for a good "sticky phrase"?

*What is celebrated is what is replicated.*

No, I'm not a poet, but I'm flattered you were thinking that.

I'm going to circle back to my giddy optimism and my belief that almost everybody wants to do a good job. I also believe that people want to be appreciated and affirmed when they do a good job. As we've discussed, part of doing a good job is living out the values of our organization.

Let's return to the example of the company that states it values innovation.

As a team member, let's say that (within the appropriate scope and space of my role) I take a step to be innovative and it fails. If my team lead comes to me and only spends time correcting me for failing in my innovation, am I going to try and be innovative again? NOT LIKELY.

Now, let's take the same example. However, this time my team lead comes and celebrates in front of our team the fact that I took the appropriate steps (within the scope of my role) to be innovative. Then my team lead offers to help me evaluate the steps I took, discusses what we can learn from it, and offers to help me in my next steps to innovate again. In this case, am I more likely to give it the good ol' college try again? YOU BET!

Why? Because what is celebrated is what is replicated.

Ready for another "sticky phrase?"

*We must share stories of culture for others to catch the culture.*

Stories help us paint a picture of how the stated and implied values are moving toward one another. Let's say I lead a non-profit in which we mobilize mentors to help youth perform better in school through tutoring. Let's also say a value of our organization is not only to tutor these students but to go "beyond tutoring" and help students know they are known and valued.

If I want people to catch that culture, then I'm sharing stories about the tutors who are going beyond tutoring to help students realize they are known and valued. I'm going to share about the tutor who showed up to a 3rd grade student's band recital, sat through the entire concert in which the trumpet section was off-key most of the time, and was willing to stay after to greet and talk to the student, the family, and to tell them all what a fantastic job the student did playing a mean clarinet.

When we share stories of culture, people will catch the culture we're trying to move toward.

**Leaders are culture creators.** And culture is created through regular rhythms over time...

In our being before our doing.

In our regular conversations.

In the things we celebrate and the stories we share.

If we want to see our stated and implied values move toward integrity, it has to start with us.

# Reflection & Discussion Questions

1. When it comes to creating culture, why is our "being" as leaders so important?

2. Why do you think it's important for leaders to use language that aligns with the culture of their organization?

3. What is one thing you could celebrate (or a story you could share) that would promote a value and the ideal culture of your organization?

# Coaching Moment

1. Ask your coach to share a value in his or her organization that is important to him or her. Ask if there is something your coach tries to do on a consistent basis to both model and encourage that value.

2. What is a value of your organization that you hold in high regard? Share that value with your coach and why it's important to you. What is one thing you can do consistently to model, encourage, and/or celebrate that value?

## 15

# KNOW YOUR TARGET

"**F**or no particular reason, I decided to go for a little run." In the 1994 film *Forrest Gump*, there is a fascinating series of scenes in which the film's namesake character, played by Tom Hanks, goes for a run that would take him across America.

Every marker of distance that Forrest meets only encourages him to run further. "For no particular reason I just kept on going," he shares. Forrest runs across the country until he meets the inevitable ocean. Upon arrival, he briefly pauses, turns around, and keeps on running!

Matched with energized music, these scenes show Forrest running through all different parts of the country. The national media even begins to take notice, and when reporters catch him on the road and ask what causes him to run, "They couldn't believe that somebody would do all that running for no particular reason."

In the film, a number of people are inspired by Forrest's venture. Some ran up alongside him and asked for advice. Others paused their lives to join him in his trek across the country. By the time his run ends, there are dozens of individuals running behind him.

Forrest ran for 3 years, 2 months, 14 days, and 16 hours. But his running journey ends pretty anticlimactically. Forrest suddenly doesn't feel like running anymore, so he stops, turns around to address his followers, and states plainly, "I'm pretty tired. I think I'll go home now."

Every time I watch this scene, I cringe a little as I see this group of runners, standing out on a road with little else in sight, *stunned* with the realization that they had really been on a road to nowhere. As Forrest walks away, one of them exclaims, "Now what are we supposed to do?!"[1]

## Where Are We Going?

It is not enough to create movement if our movement doesn't take us somewhere that matters. This is why the ability to define targets well is so valuable.

**Targets** are what we create movement toward.

Movement without a target is about the same as going for a run with no particular destination in mind. We might experience a lot of activity. Members of the organization or team might even be energized or inspired by some of the movement for a time. But if we're leading a team and asking them to move with us, shouldn't we have an idea of what we're moving toward?

This is why targets matter.

You might be thinking, "Targets sound the same as *goals*." In a sense, they are. However, targets are established not only for the purpose of accomplishing something, but also to intentionally create movement in a particular direction.

As leaders, we must have a sense of where we are taking people. If we are leading others, it's our responsibility to have spent the appropriate amount of time, strategic thinking, and prayer defining targets that will create movement toward where we want to go.

I want to be careful not to over-dramatize targets. Not every target is a massive, all-encompassing strategy. Some targets will be smaller-scale efforts of an individual or a team. But every target will impact the organization. So, whether large or small, every target should meet these five criteria:

1. It fits (the organization)

2. It points (toward a desired reality)

3. It has a plan

4. It has a next step

5. It can be measured

Let's walk through these five important criteria of a good target.

## 1. It Fits Under The Umbrella of Your Organization

As I write this, it's raining outside the window of my study in the early morning of a normal Tuesday. In a little while, as with most weekday mornings, I'll take my daughter to her bus stop for another day at school. When we take the sidewalk to her stop, I'm sure we will share an umbrella. We'll both occupy our own space under the umbrella as we move toward our intended destination. As long as we both stay underneath the umbrella, we'll avoid becoming a wet mess.

Targets must fit under the umbrella of the organization.

When we are part of an organization, we must be aware of the vision, values, processes, and practices that have already been established. As leaders, we are given space to operate underneath the organizational umbrella. However, if we step outside of the umbrella we will most likely be faced with a mess and wet with frustration.

*Here's one simple example of setting a target in your space underneath the umbrella:*

Suppose you lead a college ministry at a church that places a high value on global missions. Every year you are responsible for planning trip opportunities for college students. So, you and your team decide to establish a target of engaging students in cross-cultural mission opportunities. In establishing this target, you are operating in your space (college ministry planning) but underneath the umbrella (the missions-focused vision and values) of the organization.

This is a target that fits.

## 2. **It Points To A Desired Reality**

When establishing a target, the first question many are tempted to ask is: "What do we want to do?"

But a better question to start with is: "Where do we want to end up?"

"What is the reality we desire?"

"What would be happening in this *ideal* reality?"

"What do we want to experience?"

"Where is it that we're moving toward?"

This kind of thinking is valuable for both identifying and solving problems. And it is often leaders who are good listeners that do well at this.

A tension that is often felt in the world of church and non-profits is the constant need for volunteers. The thing about volunteer-based organizations is that there are never enough. Often different teams and departments from the same church or organization find themselves in tension, maybe even frustrated at times, as they recruit for a myriad of roles from the same base of people.

Years ago, I'd stepped into a new leadership role to lead a team in a growing organization. Early on, as I listened and investigated the experiences of people in the organization, I quickly noticed that there was some tension and misalignment between a couple teams.

These weren't personal tensions. Everybody was just trying to be faithful in his or her role on the teams. But there were differences of opinion in the best way to recruit and retain volunteers in this organization, which was continuing to grow and have even more volunteer needs.

It didn't take me long to figure out there was a desired reality we needed to create movement toward. This desired reality was that team members would have the appropriate amount of space to effectively recruit and retain volunteers in a way that fit underneath the organization's defined recruitment processes.

With this desired reality in mind, I invited the appropriate parties together where we healthily communicated the tensions we felt in our responsibilities. We worked together on an agreed upon practice that both fit the organization's process and gave space for our leaders to recruit well.

## 3. It Has A Plan

To move towards a target, you need a plan.

Having a plan means defining the specific actions you and your team believe will make the desired reality an actual reality. This is where the groundwork begins to be laid, as we establish the specific steps needed to be taken toward the target.

Let's circle back to the example of the college ministry at a church whose vision is heavily focused on world missions. Let's say the target is to see twenty-five college students engage in cross-cultural mission opportunities. We must have a plan of action steps in order to begin to move toward the target. A great way to do this is to start with the desired reality.

Then begin to work backwards, thinking through some of the steps in your plan that will help make this desired reality a realized one.

Here are some examples of the questions that might be asked:

### What is the desired reality?

*We want to see 25 college students participate in global mission trips in the next two years...*

### How many trip offerings will we need to have for these 25 college students?

*Most of our trips can include 8-9 college students, so we will need a minimum of 3 trip opportunities...*

### Where are these opportunities found?

*Our church partners with a number of ministries in different global locations. We'll work with our Missions Department to discuss potential trips and to define logistics such as cost.*

### How will the expenses for these trips be covered?

### Who will lead these trips?

### How will college students apply for trips?

### What is the most effective way to encourage college students to apply to attend a trip?

If we want to move toward our target then we must have a plan of action.

## 4. It Has A Next Step

As I've seen, watched, and talked with different leaders, I have come to appreciate the many and often daunting steps it takes to move toward targets, and it can often take a long time to reach those targets.

In a "Let's make it happen right now" culture, I admire the resiliency and patience of seasoned leaders who take the appropriate amount of time to follow the right steps for the benefit of the organization long-term.

In the world of church leadership, consider all that ministry leaders must do. They not only establish targets, but they are often the ones building infrastructure and processes for those targets. As those are being put in place, they recruit, train, and empower staff and volunteers towards the targets of the God-given vision their faith community is called to.

All of these things don't just happen. Behind the curtain of ministry leadership there is heavy toil and long hours of work bathed in prayer. Thus, many ministry leaders I've talked to have echoed the sentiment, "If people only knew!"

And while all of these things do happen, they don't happen all at once. They are often a result of steps being taken… one at a time. Often all we have is the next step, and often that is enough.

In fact, too many options or potential steps can be overwhelming and challenging. We might feel "paralyzed" to a degree or concerned that we won't make the best or "right" step. Sometimes we just have to be okay with just getting to the next step.

*So, what is a practical way to plan our next steps?*

My friends Geoff and Sherry Surratt coach many church and ministry leaders throughout the country.[2] They've even worked with some of our team from Lifepoint Church, the church I currently serve on staff with at the time of this writing. One of the practices they recommend is for leaders to create 18-month timelines for strategic goals (a.k.a. *targets*). Then they have leaders break them down in 6-month blocks.

Each 6-month block should have a defined step for your team to take, and it should include:

- What your team will do

- Which team member will lead that step

- The date that step will be complete by

- How you will measure success

After those six months, the team will get together, measure and evaluate the step you took, and define the next step together. This is a great approach, and I encourage you to utilize it when faced with your next target that requires multiple steps!

## 5. It Can Be Measured By Metrics & Stories

How do we measure whether we have moved toward or reached the target we established?

Evaluation can often include metrics (data). Or it might include stories that reflect realization of the target. In my conversations with different leaders, I've learned that some will naturally lean towards metrics for evaluation, while others are going to lean towards stories—and often their leaning reflects how they are wired as a person and leader.

What I recommend, especially for church and ministry leaders, is to combine both metrics and stories in evaluating whether you're moving toward the target. We usually *feel* stories, but we must also value the data and metrics. Without it, we might allow stories to unintentionally warp our view of the whole based on how the story makes us feel.

A friend of mine once told me that there is both an art and science to measuring health. I think the same can be said about measuring movement.

*Here's a practical example…*

Suppose a team of ten people, including myself, launch a small group in our community.

And say that we have established a target of multiplying that group into 6 more small groups (of 10 people each), each led by a capable leader, in the next 3 years.

Now, suppose that after a year we have launched only 1 other group, and the original group has only 8 people participating on a weekly basis.

The metric might show that we are behind in moving toward the target of launching groups since we should have launched 2 groups by now. However, the story might tell us that there are 3 leaders who have been trained and equipped and are ready to launch their own groups in the next 3 months.

Now flip the script.

Suppose that after a year, I have launched 4 groups, but I'm leading each group myself. While the metrics show that I am technically ahead of schedule in one aspect of the target, the story tells me that I'm behind in training and equipping capable leaders.

Both the metric and the story matter when measuring movement.

Early on in leadership, the metrics and data will often be easier to read and understand, but we will probably need help in measuring the stories. As one seasoned ministry leader puts it, "It takes experience to measure the art side. Until you've arrived at a certain level of experience, lean on people who have the experience."

## Move In A Particular Direction

I think back to that group of people standing on the road in the middle of nowhere as Forrest Gump walked away. All of that running and activity—only to be left standing with no destination in mind.

May we be careful to not just lead people but to help them move in a particular direction.

As leaders we have the responsibility to be diligent and thoughtful in the targets that we and our teams establish. As we operate in our space, which is underneath the umbrella of our organization, we must consider where we actually want to end up.

We must be planners. We must consider what actions, including the next step, we should take. We must take the time to honestly measure our movement, re-evaluate, and then decide the next step toward the target.

In so doing, we'll create movement toward where we actually want to go.

## Reflection & Discussion Questions

1. Why is it important for a target to fit within the vision and values of an organization?

2. Why is being a good listener important for establishing the right targets?

3. Why is prayer so valuable for establishing the right targets?

4. Are you more likely to lean toward using metrics or stories when it comes to measuring successful movement towards a target? Why do you think that is?

# Coaching Moment

1. Ask your coach to share a best practice he or she has learned as it comes to defining targets (goals) well.

2. Share with your coach a current, defined target you have in place and ask him or her to help you evaluate it (utilizing the material from this chapter). Is there a way to better clarify or define that target?

# 16

# FOLLOW THE MAPS

I can still remember the moment I passed my driver's exam and received my license for the first time. I was sixteen years old and had finally reached a whole new level of independence. I was no longer reliant on family members or friends for transportation and could finally drive myself.

My grandmother gave me my first car. It was a used, blue 1993 Oldsmobile Cutlass Ciera. You probably just checked to see what that car looks like on Google. Yes, that seemingly oversized sardine tin on wheels was my first car. And that old car, combined with my new license, were the keys to my freedom of going where I wanted to go.

However, while I quickly embraced my newfound independence, I would soon realize that I had a problem: I had an awful sense of direction.

When I began driving, I realized that for my entire life I'd relied on others to know where to go and which roads to take.

Places I'd visited on numerous occasions were now a struggle to find, and navigating the roads that led to others seemed confusing.

Not understanding the specific roads to take resulted in any road being an option, but I had no clarity about which was the *right* road. This was actually antithetical to the freedom I'd hoped for, and it was paralyzing. Looking back, I realize the significant amount of time, energy, and mental effort I spent just trying to figure out the best road to take, and I often felt insecure and frustrated because I didn't really have clarity on my route.

To help, my father began drawing out maps for me. He would draw specific directions for how to get to where I needed. He would draw lines for roads, label them, and even noted landmarks to be aware of. Soon enough, in the glovebox of my old, blue car sat a small stack of maps that I could refer back to. These maps gave me clarity about the right routes to take so I could get where I really wanted to go without getting lost or frustrated.

To this day I can still struggle with directions from time to time. So, I'm really thankful for the technological advancements that provide us maps on our phones and other GPS devices in our vehicles. I am also thankful for the app on my phone that allows me to plug in my desired destination and gives me different route options, which will keep me on the correct paths and within the right parameters.

For someone who is directionally challenged, maps are a game-changer. They give me clarity for the route that leads me to my target. For the Christian leader, having clarity for how we want to move toward our targets is necessary as well. This is why we need to follow our maps.

# Why Maps Matter

In the last chapter, I introduced the idea of *targets*, the desired realities we create movement toward. Now we're going to discuss defining the routes to move toward those targets.

More often than not, everybody wants to reach the same target, but people often have differing ideas and opinions on the best path to get there. Without clear pathways and parameters, there is risk for members of a team or organization to start heading in different directions. This can result in frustration, misalignment, and even paralysis that keep teams and organizations from moving toward where they truly want to go. This is why *maps*—and keeping to them—are necessary.

**Maps** are the defined paths and parameters in which team members move towards the target. They provide clarity and space for team members to work and move. They also establish guardrails to keep team members on track, rather than ending up on a path that actually leads away from where they are trying to go.

The best *maps* are driven by the intersection of two, necessary *coordinates*, if you will.

### 1. They support the vision and values of the organization

Team members should have a general, yet clear sense of "this is what we do" or "this is how we function here" as active participants of their organization. Clear parameters for those members of an organization help people to understand "this is who we are and how we work together."

A good map when it comes to how members functions within their organization might be a "Code of Conduct." More than just a set of rules, a good code of conduct gives clarity for how team members will relate to and work with one another.

Another practical map is a "Staff Flow Chart" that helps people to understand who leads certain areas of responsibility and decision-making and how team members function within the organization hierarchy.

### 2. They apply to a defined target

Team members should not only have clarity for "how we work and move" but also understand the consistent things we are going to do to help move in the direction of a particular target.

I like to call these consistent tasks, *tactics*. These are a primary driver in movement. Team members should have clarity for the consistent tasks they are responsible for and how they fit the defined targets of the team and organization.

In leading one ministry team, one of the things I learned was that just asking a volunteer to lead a weekly small group was not enough. Even though our target of having small groups that cultivated effective discipleship was clear, leaving leaders to the simple ask and expectation of "lead a small group" was insufficient. It could result in a dozen small groups that all looked completely different and misaligned in the *way* that they could be led. So, another key leader and I developed a job description for our small group leaders and a guide that laid out the key elements of group time and their purpose. We also built interactive, training time around both the job description and the guide.

In doing so, we created *maps* that provided clarity and parameters in which our team members could lead their groups well and in a way that was clear and consistent for every group in the ministry.

## The Everyday Things Matter Most

The most valuable efforts in reaching targets are the everyday and consistent tasks and tactics of the organization's people. It is these everyday tasks and weekly rhythms that ultimately move teams and organizations in a particular direction. There should be clarity as to not only what we and team members should be doing but also about the "how" of doing it within clear paths and parameters.

All the things our team members do on a consistent basis should point back to our vision, values, and targets. In my experience, team members are usually more energized and committed to their efforts if they have a sense of how it points back to the vision of our team and organization.

Often when we desire to "speed up" movement, we add supplemental efforts. This might be an event, conference, campaign, or special program. There is nothing wrong with having supplemental efforts to catalyze movement as long as the supplemental effort fits three criteria:

1. It fits the within the parameters and pathways of your team and organization (a.k.a. the maps!)

2. It contributes to movement toward an already defined target that is tethered to your consistent tactics. (*Never create a short-term, temporary target just to justify an idea, program, event, or other effort.)

3. It does not compete with or compromise the primary, consistent tactics.

*Here's a practical example…*

Say your organization was considering hosting a weekend conference to educate, resource, and support married couples. In itself, that is a good effort. But is it the right effort for your organization? Consider these kinds of questions to see if it fits your *map*:

- Does this effort fit the stated vision, values, and targets of your organization?

- Does it apply to your consistent tactics and rhythms over time?

- Does your organization have a long-term, consistent pathway, infrastructure, and community for these couples to be supported long-term?

- Do you have dedicated staff or leaders (paid or volunteer) that can be a resource to and support these couples over time?

- Are you connected with local counselors you can refer couples to?

- Do you have financial means to potentially subsidize those counseling costs?

While our motivations might be honorable, could the reality be that we are inviting these couples to attend this event and be provided with good information, resources, and a helpful experience only to have no consistent pathway for them to be supported for more than a weekend?

If not, as a married person I can tell you hosting an event without being able to support my wife and me long-term doesn't really seem fair. As someone who has led teams of staff and volunteers, I'd be concerned that asking them to host this might not be a wise way to steward individuals who will give their time and effort for something that has such short-term movement.

The truth of the matter is that our efforts have to make sense within the vision, values, targets, and consistent tactics of our organization—not compete with them. This will help us avoid being a poor steward of time, finances, and our most valuable resource: the people whom we are entrusted to lead. If there is ever a place where there is temptation to do this, it is in the world of churches...

## Know Your Best No

After serving in a number of churches over the years, I have come to realize that everybody has good ideas. Really, everybody does. If I had a dollar for every conversation I had with somebody that centered on a good idea, I'd probably be able to retire early...really early.

I've had tons of discussions initiated by suggestions from good people about different kinds of events, programs, and efforts that folks would like to see happen. These have been conversations with volunteers, church members, and staff employees. Much of these conversations I've had have been centered around ideas I've suggested myself!

In reality, though, it is often a small percentage of our ideas that actually fit the *map* of the organization. Don't get me wrong—these are almost always good ideas! But often, only select ideas are the right ideas that truly fit the vision, values, and the defined targets of our team and organization.

Christian leader, it is paramount that we have clarity for the kinds of the things, ideas, and opportunities we'll say "yes" to. It is even more important to know what we'll say "no" to.

When it comes to suggested ideas that don't necessarily fit the map of a team and organization, I've come to realize that pain is almost always inevitable. We just have to choose the better pain.

The better pain is the short-term pain where we say, "I really appreciate you bringing that idea. It sounds like a wonderful effort, but it just doesn't fit us and where we're moving right now."

Saying this can be painful—for them and for us. But it is often short-term pain. Yes, it is going to be a withdrawal in your relational passbook with that individual. However, it will protect everyone from long-term pain.

Long-term pain comes when we say yes to something that is a deviation from our *map*. It's when we say "yes" to something that doesn't fit the vision, values, and targets of our organization, as well as our consistent tactics and rhythms.

When we say "yes" to what we should have said "no" to, it quickly snowballs into asking people to give time, energy, effort, and other resources to a work that really doesn't fit the collective. Then we're stuck with resources being allocated to an effort that is way off track of our map.

What seems like a small deviation in the short term ends up becoming a large deviation over time. These small compromises can often lead to big collapses. Think of a sinkhole. A small leak in a pipe, over time, becomes a complete collapse of a large area and creates major damage.

Sometimes the most difficult "no" is the one team members have to say to each other. In fact, I've experienced teammates respond to some of my suggestions with a kind but clear "no" and then explain why my suggestion didn't fit the map.

Did I experience some frustration there? Absolutely. Did it hurt my pride in the short-term? Heck yea, it did. But looking back, I recognize that their best "no" helped keep me, our team, and our organization from doing something that would have gotten us off track and outside of our map. Often the best "no" is the one we say to other team members because it helps us to better collectively guard the vision, values, and the culture of our organization. It also saves the collective team from future pain.

## How We Create History

*A friendly warning to those serving in leadership in a church, ministry, or non-profit...*

When something is "tried out" once, immediately a history has been created for that effort. This means there are at least a few people who now have investment in that effort. As soon as something has history and investment, any attempt to end that effort means pain and a significant relational withdrawal for somebody.

This pain is often more amplified in the world of the church and ministry. Why? Because often people who love Jesus and are part of his church have big hearts! That's a reason I love serving in the church—the people, their big heats, and their zeal for the Kingdom! However, when our big hearts get tethered to something we consider meaningful and then somebody tries to take that away, it hurts. This is why so many churches continue to host and invest in some of the same yearly events, campaigns, and programs that don't truly contribute to any movement: because few leaders want to embrace the pain of saying "no" to something that has so much history and investment!

Christian leader, we often spare other people and ourselves greater pain when we choose the better pain of saying "no" to something that doesn't fit the map of our organization.

• • •

Whenever I step onto the staff team of a church, I'm always fascinated to hear the early history of how God brought the leaders together and led them through the process of clearly defining the vision and values of that local body of His church. When I get to have these kinds of conversations, there are often stories in which good, godly leaders have had to make very difficult decisions in order to stay aligned with their God-given vision and values.

This is why I appreciate my friends who are church planters. They have an incredible call and gifting that is driven by God's vision of His church being extended throughout the world and in our communities.

As someone who thinks more like an executive than a visionary, do I sometimes think they're nuts to take on such a seemingly risky mission and work? Absolutely.

Do they have my upmost respect for how they step out in faith and obedience to what God is asking them to do? Absolutely—times a million!

Troy Palermo, the Executive Pastor at Lifepoint Church (where I currently serve on staff), was and is part of the core team of leaders who planted and founded the church. In talking with him about the history of planting Lifepoint, he shared that there have been numerous times where really great, godly people came to leadership with good ideas. However, those ideas weren't the right ideas for the vision and values that leadership felt God had given to them. And so, leadership had to say "no."

The right "no" definitely meant pain. Some of these good people walked away from the church because they weren't given a path to move outside of the map. This meant pain, not only for those individuals but also for the church planters who desired to have these great, godly people be part of what God was calling them to do. And frankly, when planting a church, we need people! But I give the leadership of Lifepoint credit for being wise enough to know and say the right "no," even if it meant short-term pain.

**In order to avoid long-term pain,** we must understand, follow, and guard the *maps* of our teams and organization. We must have clarity about the pathways and parameters in which we can move. The efforts that matter most are the everyday tactics and weekly rhythms that continually point back to our vision, values, and defined targets. While it is good to have supplemental efforts, we must make sure those efforts contribute, and not compete against, the consistent tasks and rhythms that matter most.

The reality is that in order to lead people and teams well we are going to have to know our best "no." But in reality, saying "no" means saying "yes." We're saying "yes" to staying within the map and on the right paths that will help us move toward where we actually want to go.

## Reflection & Discussion Questions

1. In your own words, how would you describe a *map*?

2. Why do our everyday tasks and weekly rhythms matter more than our short-term, supplemental efforts?

3. Explain why a small, short-term deviation from our paths and parameters can easily become a large deviation over time?

4. Is it difficult for you to say no to others? Why or why not?

## Coaching Moment

1. Ask your coach to share an example of having to give his or her best "no" to somebody. What was said "no" to and why?

2. Share with your coach if you often find it difficult to say "no" to people or not. Why do you think that is? As you share, listen to see if there might be an inward fear that is keeping you from giving your best "no" when it is necessary.

# 17

# LEADING TEAMS WELL

I have always been fascinated by the concept of "the team."
Even in my youth, as I watched my favorite sports teams
compete, I always appreciated how much more a team
could accomplish when compared with an individual.

Don't get me wrong. There's something to be said for
individuals who have been given great talent. When the
Cleveland Cavaliers won the NBA Championship in 2016,
without a doubt LeBron James was the best player on the
floor. And he deservedly won the award for Most Valuable
Player of the NBA Finals.

But while individuals earn accolades, teams win
championships.

As great as LeBron was in that series, the team wouldn't
have won that championship if only LeBron had played. In
fact, significant contributions came from his teammates.

The head coach, Tyron Lue, who was thrust into his role halfway through the season, was a key catalyst in putting together a game plan that stymied the record-setting Golden State Warriors' high-tempo offense.

In addition, Kyrie Irving helped with a large portion of the scoring throughout the series, which included making a three-point basket near the end of the series' final game that gave the Cavaliers a lead and the chance to win.

After Kyrie made his "three-pointer," power forward Kevin Love had to defend league MVP Steph Curry. Love, who was mismatched against the smaller, quicker Curry, played perfect defense, forcing him to miss his shot to the basket.

Many other players on the Cavaliers made significant contributions, not only in game seven, but throughout the series. It took every team member for the Cavaliers to become the first team in NBA history to come back from a three-games-to-one deficit in a best of seven playoff series. They also were the first franchise from Cleveland to win a major professional sports championship in 52 years!

LeBron was great. But it took the team to win.

## The 5 C's Of Leading Teams

I'm regrettably not much of an athlete, but I'm very passionate about **teams**. It takes the collective, a team, to accomplish far more than individuals can on their own. At the same time, I've never seen a team win without effective leadership.

I'd like to share with you five principles I've learned about leading teams well. Whether you lead a small group, a team of staff at work, or a team of volunteers at a church, *"The 5 C's of Leading Teams"* can apply to you.

## 1. **Consistency**

As leaders, it is imperative to be consistent. Our consistency, not only in our moods, but also in the way we treat and interact with team members, is important. Why? Because it's not fair to ask team members to guess what they should expect from us each day.

Sometimes we learn what we should do by experiencing what *not* to do. If you've ever had a leader or boss who leaves you wondering what to expect each day, well, it's a miserable experience. We find ourselves walking on eggshells and trying to guess what kind of mood they're in or how they'll respond to a decision we make. It's completely debilitating as a team member. Let's not subject that misery on those we lead.

Being consistent does not mean that we always "have it all together." We can have consistency in our temperament and in the posture of our interactions while at the same having appropriate transparency on the days that we aren't doing well.

A few years ago, I was leading a weekend retreat, and on the morning of the final day, my family reached out to tell me that my grandmother had passed away during the night. My grandmother and I were very close. She had been battling cancer for years, and it had been a painful process to watch her suffer and see her health and mental state deteriorate over time.

That morning a slew of emotions rushed through my heart and mind. A couple members of our leadership team knew what had happened and asked me how I was doing. I shared that I was sad and hurting. However, I knew the group still needed me to lead the rest of the time. In the midst of not doing well, I asked God for the grace to be consistent and lead the group well for the rest of the time. God was gracious in giving me strength that I wouldn't have had on my own that day.

## 2. **Communication**

In the same way that we should be clear about what team members can expect from us, we should also be clear in communicating what is expected of them. Being specific and even writing (or typing) down the specific expectations, responsibilities, and tasks that each team member is responsible for helps provide this clarity.

In communication with team members, it always helpful when we can communicate with people using mediums that are helpful for the group overall, even if those mediums are a little outside of our comfort zone. The reality is that there are certain methods of communication that we will personally prefer. However, as leaders we ought to be willing to put aside personal preferences if it helps us to communicate to the team better overall. This is just another example of how we can be servant leaders.

There are often generational trends regarding preferred methods of communication. *The Human Resources Professional Association* published a report that highlighted some of these generational trends.[1] While these might not be true of everyone, research tells us these are the general trends of generational communication preferences in the workplace:

- *Traditionalists* (born between 1900-1945) prefer written communication.

- *Baby Boomers* (born between 1946-1964) prefer personal interaction and verbal communication. "Ok, Boomer." Sorry—I had to.

- *Generation X* (born between 1965-1980) often prefers email or voicemail.

- *Generation Z*, often known as Millennials, (born between 1977-1994) prefers text messages, instant message, and email.

Being cognizant of who is on your team and what communication method is most beneficial for the team (and not just for our preference) will help us communicate more effectively.

Communication not only involves our methods, but our posture as well. You may have heard of the famous "7-38-55 rule" based on the research of UCLA psychology professor Albert Mehrian.[2] His theory is that personal communication is:

- 7% spoken words

- 38% voice and tone

- 55% body language

Communication is not only what people hear or read. It's also what they see and feel.

One of the ways leaders can evaluate and grow in our communication ability is by learning to be a student of others. What do we see in people's eyes, face, and posture as we communicate? What might that tell us about how they are receiving what we are communicating?

One of the things I've learned about myself is that when I'm very focused, including during communication or a discussion with team members, I sometimes have what I call a "resting concerned face." This natural posture and facial expression (abbreviation "RCF") is where my eyebrows are low, my face is stern, and I actually look somewhat concerned.

I've noticed that team members will actually shift what or how they're sharing something with me when they see my RCF. My actual intent is to give team members my attention and focus while processing what they're sharing. However, my "resting concerned face" communicates to them that I don't understand or necessarily like what they're saying and that I'm concerned by it—which, again, is completely opposite of my intent!

As I grow in being a student of others, I'm learning to replace my habit of RCF in my interactions and communication with others. Another leader shared with me his practice of "Eyebrows Up!" The idea is that, when talking and interacting with team members, we talk with our eyebrows up, which communicates a kinder and more engaging disposition as people share. I'm working on it. What in your posture do you need to work on when communicating?

## 3. Care

For years, families were invited into the television home of their favorite neighbor, Fred Rogers. One of the most famous episodes of *Mister Rogers' Neighborhood* featured a young boy named Jeff Erlanger in an electric wheelchair. Jeff had significant disabilities and was about to have an especially difficult spinal injury. However, his parents wanted him to be able to meet his favorite television friend, so Jeff went on the show and had an incredible conversation with Mister Rogers that was both unscripted and unrehearsed.

During the conversation, two things quickly became clear as Fred asked questions and Jeff shared about his many physical difficulties. First, Jeff was a remarkable boy—articulate, joyful, and kind in the midst of great trials. And second, Fred Rogers was a shining example of how we should treat every person with value and care, no matter how different.[3]

As the segment closed, Fred and Jeff sang together. The song they sang was a popular, regular song on the show. It's a simple, yet profound song called, "It's You I Like." The lyrics are as follows:

*It's you I like,*
*It's not the things you wear,*
*It's not the way you do your hair--*
*But it's you I like.*
*The way you are right now,*

*The way down deep inside you--*
*Not the things that hide you,*
*Not your toys--*
*They're just beside you.*

*But it's you I like--*
*Every part of you,*
*Your skin, your eyes, your feelings*
*Whether old or new.*
*I hope that you'll remember*
*Even when you're feeling blue*
*That it's you I like,*
*It's you yourself,*
*It's you, it's you I like.*[4]

People have to know that they are valued. In leading team members, we should be the first to communicate to others that they are valuable. I'm sure Mister Rogers had his bad days, but I've never seen or heard of him not treating people with care. May we be so intentional, even on our worst days, to speak and treat people well and with care.

### 4. **Collaboration**

As it relates to teams, the expert is not in the room—the expert *is* the room.

Leaders who lead out of a vacuum—who move without inviting the right team members into the conversation, asking good questions, and considering their perspectives, experiences, and expertise—usually find themselves frustrated and frustrating team members. Leaders who lead teams well are almost always good collaborators.

Collaboration is when two or more people work together to create or achieve the same thing.[5]

And it is the responsibility of leaders to provide space and opportunity for collaboration. We do this by inviting team members into conversations that have to do with the efforts that match their current organizational role, experience, or expertise.

When an organization's leadership team is smaller, often those team members naturally have to wear "multiple hats." The natural result is that these leaders are often part of many different collaborative conversations because their responsibilities connect with many different efforts of the organization.

As organizations grow, it usually becomes increasingly difficult for every team member to be part of every organizational decision. This is a normal tension. It's not that the input of every team member isn't valuable. It's just logically unrealistic for every team member's valuable input to be considered in all the decision-making.

When this happens, leaders often learn to target *who* is invited to collaborate on *what*. Like the children's toy of matching shaped blocks to their correct counterpart holes, leaders learn to match team members with the appropriate discussions, efforts, and decisions based on team members' roles, experience, expertise, and opportunity.

Some organizations do a good job of establishing teams based on the intersection of team members' primary responsibilities. Then, these organizations create a regular rhythm of meeting in order for those teams to collaborate within their areas of primary responsibility. For organizations that don't do this well, there is often the natural tendency for most team members to expect the opportunity to participate in any or most of the collaboration and decision-making discussions.

## 5. **Courage**

When I was a student pastor, each year we took our students on a summer trip. Many of these were mission trips. Over time, it organically became an expectation that our student trips meant taking a long road trip to a new city in order to partner with local ministries in those cities. Toronto, New Orleans, and Kansas City were among some of the cities to which we traveled.

One year, during the fall, I began planning one of these future summer trips. I began by praying and asking God where He would have us go. In the process of researching, collaborating with team members, and listening to God speak, it became increasingly clear to me how important it was for our ministry to not just go great distances to serve, but also that we ought to bear the burden of serving neighbors who were closer to home as well.

As I continued to pray, one particular city kept coming back to mind: Canton, Ohio. Malone University, where I went to college, was there. Spending four years in the community gave me awareness of some of the substantial physical and spiritual needs of the community. I was also aware of some of the fantastic ministries in the city with whom we could partner.

So, I took all the necessary steps within our ministry's map:

- I collaborated with our team.

- I communicated and was on the same page with leadership.

- I took the extra step of taking some of our adult and student leaders for a day-trip to visit and meet with the local ministries we would partner with in the city.

- We brought back metrics, stories, and even video of the ministries to help our students *catch the vision* for the trip.

I took all of the seemingly right steps as a leader. And you know what? There were people who were unhappy with me. Some told me directly. Others didn't. But I knew that there was disappointment because we were only going down the road to Canton, Ohio.

In fairness, for students from Cleveland, going to Canton is about as exciting as leaving your hometown, driving around for an hour, and ending up in the same place you started.

To this day, I don't blame those students for their disappointment.

I would have been disappointed too.

I had taken all the right steps and followed all the right processes as a leader. At this point, there was really one thing left to do—have courage.

Courage, in this case, meant sticking to my conviction that this is where we should go and serve without the promise of being able to please everyone or that the trip would go smoothly.

I believe that when God gives us a role of leadership He not only is using us to serve and help others, but He also uses others to help us. In this case, He was using others to help me grow in courage.

*I guess you want to know what happened on the trip.*

Well, it was AWESOME. To this day, I have students who tell me it was the best summer trip they ever went on. We served faithfully and helped local individuals and families connect with long-term ministries in the area. We also helped and supported brothers and sisters in Christ who were living in and are having an impact on the city of Canton.

During the week, we gained a real sense of the unity of the greater church—it felt palpable. The collective group of leaders across the partnering ministries were from different backgrounds, races, and denominations, and yet we were all unified by Christ and a Spirit-led connection that only believers can grasp.

Our student ministry became closer relationally and bonded together during that trip. As we served together during the hot summer days, we experienced joy and laughter together. In the evenings—when we met to share, debrief, and pray as a group—there was a very real sense of togetherness. In our interactions, it was clear that we were *for* each other and that God was doing many things in and through us.

Over years of ministry, I've lost count of the number of retreats, conferences camps, and mission trips I've been part of or led. But this one was different. The day I came home from the trip, I sat with my wife in our family room to share about the trip, and I began to weep. And I mean, I *sobbed*. My wife, absolutely shocked to see me cry (it's not something I do often), asked me if I was okay. Through my tears I was able to share two things:

1. I was humbled and grateful that God would be so good to work in and through our team in the way He did during the week.

2. I was proud of our team, especially our students. The way they served, cared for people, and cared for each other...I was just so proud of them.

When you value and care for the people you lead and when you lead in order to see the team do greater things, your joy doesn't come from anything you do. It comes from seeing what the team does—together. And sometimes, in order for that to happen, you need courage.

When you win together, nobody really cares who gets to hold the trophy.

What matters is that you won together.

**If we want to really "win,"** then we must lead teams well. We do this by...

- Being **consistent**, so that team members have clear expectations about what to expect from us.

- **Communicating** clearly so that team members know what is expected from them.

- Showing team members that we **care** for and value them.

- **Collaborating** in order for the team to create and achieve together.

- Having **courage** when we must lead from conviction.

And always remember: individuals earn accolades, but it is the team who wins.

## Reflection & Discussion Questions

1. How can a leader's inconsistency be detrimental for team members?

2. What are practical ways a leader can communicate that he or she values team members?

3. How would you define "courage"?

## Coaching Moment

1. Ask your coach to share a tip or best practice he or she has learned as it comes to leading a team or group well.

2. Glance over *The 5 C's of Leading Teams* and share with your coach which of those you would like to improve in. In what way would your development in that area benefit your team? What opportunity or resource might be available to help develop in that way?

# 18

# TAKE TIME TO CELEBRATE

Have you ever heard the classic song "Celebration" by Kool and the Gang? If you get the chance, play the song on a device or just let what you remember of the song play in your head. (See, I told you classic songs were the best.)

Go ahead—let your toe tap.

There you go.

You can let your head bob a little.

Don't be afraid to sing-a-long if you'd like.

We're not celebrating your being so close to finishing this book. (However, congratulations on making it to this point!)

No—we're celebrating *celebration* itself.

Have you ever watched a team accomplish a great feat?

Maybe the team set a new record or had a winning streak of some kind?

Maybe they defeated a highly favored opponent?

Maybe they won a championship?

What happens after? They celebrate!

Confetti flies through the air. Teammates high five and hug. Everybody kisses the trophy, which—now that I think about it—is pretty gross and unsanitary. Somebody yells on camera, "I'm going to Disney World!" Players are interviewed by reporters. It is in these moments the players and coaches begin to reflect on and share all that they were able to accomplish...together.

And it makes sense. When a team arrives at the target they've moved towards together, celebration is the only logical response.

## Why We Celebrate

Celebration is an incredibly valuable habit of leadership. However, it's also an often-forgotten habit of leadership. Whether we're celebrating the faithful efforts of our team, when our team reaches a target, or when an individual contributes to the greater good of the team and organization, we need to take time to celebrate.

Here are three things that happen when we take time to celebrate:

### 1. Value Is Communicated

As mentioned before, what is celebrated reveals what is valued. But also, *who* is celebrated communicates *who* is valued. If we value our team and its members, then we will celebrate them and their efforts.

### 2. The Team Benefits

Two words: "Positive reinforcement." People want to not only know that they are valued but also that they are appreciated. When leaders take the time to appreciate the hard work, effort, and faithfulness of team members, it often brings energy and motivation to continue to be faithful and to contribute.

### 3. It Reminds Us That We Are Servant Leaders

When we, as leaders, pause to make sure that our team is celebrated well, it can often help to remind us that we serve our teammates. Remember, a servant leader leads for the benefit of others. Even if we have a team member who handles the logistics of the celebration, when we pause to contemplate how we can best celebrate, appreciate, and encourage our team then we are serving them.

## Ways We Celebrate

There are different ways in which we can celebrate our teams and its members.

### 1. By Having A Regular Rhythm of Celebration

One of the easiest ways to make sure that we *do* celebrate is by having a regular rhythm of celebration. What kinds of things could you put on the calendar that would give you an opportunity to celebrate your team?

A lot of leaders like to schedule a Christmas party or dinner for their teams. What might be the best time of the year for your team based on the rhythm of your team's calendar?

Or, how might you incorporate appreciation efforts into the gatherings you already have scheduled? Do you have a regular rhythm of meeting with your team? What if you took time during those meetings to celebrate specific efforts of the team and its members?

### 2. Irregular Times of Celebration

Daisies and Reese's peanut butter cups. Those are my wife's favorite kind of flower and her favorite candy. And you know what? She really appreciates when I bring her those as a way of telling her I love her and appreciate her. But what if the only time I ever brought her flowers and candy was Valentine's Day? Would that communicate that I'm a genuinely appreciative husband? Probably not. While she still appreciates my celebrating her on Valentine's Day, I've learned that it's the times I unexpectedly bring her these tokens of affection that she feels even more valued.

As leaders, we should be on the lookout for irregular times when we can celebrate and appreciate our teams. Whether it be taking team members to lunch, taking time to appreciate a team member who might have reached a particular career milestone, or pausing to recognize when our team reached a target, these "out-of-the-normal-rhythm" celebrations help team members feel appreciated.

Not always, but often a good time to intentionally appreciate or encourage the team is either during or right after a challenging season. This might be a strenuous time in which team members have extra responsibilities. Or this might be when surprise situations arise and team members have to quickly adjust and make key decisions based on new information. I've always been thankful for leaders who have a good handle on the art of knowing when their team needs encouragement and appreciation or when they just need time and space to take next steps.

## How To Celebrate Well

So, how do we celebrate and appreciate team members well?

### 1. **Be Excellent**

We communicate value not only in our celebrating but also in *how* we celebrate team members. Remember, excellence is doing the best you can with what you have. We should do the same with our celebration efforts.

Suppose you're hosting an appreciation event for a team of volunteers. Utilize what resources you have to do it well. Whether you have $100 or $1,000 budgeted for that event, utilize what you have to communicate to team members how much they are valued.

Let's say you decide to order pizza for everyone. If you order pizza, make sure that it is *good* pizza. Don't be like Michael Scott from *The Office*, who bought his staff team lunch from *Pizza By Alfredo* (which everybody found disgusting) just because it was cheaper.[1] Saving a few dollars on awful pizza does not equal good stewardship. It means you wasted money on pizza nobody wants to eat.

Remember that logistics matter. What was meant to be an effort to appreciate team members can unintentionally become a draining obligation for them because we didn't think through how logistics might impact their experience. Make sure you have enough food and seating. Think through whether team members have children and how the timing of your event might impact childcare. And please, don't make the event painfully long. Make it long enough so that people felt it was worth their time, but always leave them wanting a little more.

Now, what I'm about to tell you may be the most important piece of advice I give in regard to celebration. Don't miss this next part. When it comes to celebrating your team... MAKE IT FUN. Humans have this innate tendency to take ourselves and what we do too seriously sometimes. Provide a space for people to enjoy, smile, and laugh together.

Some of us leaders aren't great at making things fun. We're just not. On the "fun scale," I'm probably a 6 or 7, just above average. Maybe you're like me or even lower. That is okay. You know why? I bet someone on your team is an 8 or a 9.

A few years ago, I led a leadership team that included Brittany, one of the most gifted leaders I know when it comes to relational leadership and *fun*. Every year, we hosted a

Christmas party to celebrate and appreciate our team. When we planned the event, guess who I asked to plan and lead the "fun" elements of the party? You guessed correctly—Brittany. And she knocked it out of the park. By the end of the event, everybody was smiling ear to ear and laughing together as we participated in the fun elements she led.

### 2. Point Back to The Greater Vision

Leverage times of celebration to point back to the greater vision of your team and organization. In appreciating team members, help them to see why they and their faithful efforts matter in where you're moving toward.

A couple of years ago, one of our children's ministry directors had the great idea to interview a few of our parents during our annual appreciation event for our volunteer leaders. Parents shared stories of how our church's children's ministry team had an impact on the lives of their children who were now growing up and following Jesus.

Then our director asked the volunteer leaders who cared for these children when they were babies to stand. Then she asked the same thing of leaders who cared for the children when they were preschoolers. You think those leaders caught the vision of why their faithfulness over time in leading, caring, and praying for these young ones mattered? Absolutely.

Finally, if you lead in the church or a Christian organization, we must be intentional to celebrate God's activity and to praise Him for using what is ultimately His team for His Kingdom and glory. You and I know nothing happens without His kind and gracious hand at work. May we give Him the best of our celebration.

# Be An Encourager

Celebration shouldn't just happen when the team is all together. It can happen in the seemingly small moments of encouraging and affirming team members. Here are three, simple tips for doing this well:

## 1. Be Intentional

Celebrating and encouraging teammates doesn't happen accidentally. We must be intentional to look for opportunities to encourage and affirm team members. Think of it as having your "encourager-antennae" up.

## 2. Be Specific

Encouragements and affirmations matter much more when they are specific. Saying, "Jacob, you're doing a great job" doesn't matter as much as, "Jacob, I really appreciate how you lead this effort in this specific way" or "Thanks for bringing this specific idea to the team. It will greatly benefit us in this way."

## 3. Give Credit Where It Is Due

When someone on your team contributes something that is noticed by others and someone says to you, "You did a great job on this," or "This was good work by your team," we ought to be quick to give credit where it is due. Respond with something like, "Thanks. Really, it was Ella's idea. It was great thinking on her part" or, "Thanks. Ella did the vast majority of the work leading that effort. She really knocked it out of the park." When it comes to the team, should we really be worried about who gets the credit if we all win? Not necessarily. However, I think we show integrity as a leader when we give credit where it is due. If we're servant leaders, we're serving for the benefit of others. So, we should be glad when others are celebrated for their excellence.

**Take time to celebrate.** May you and I not forget what a valuable leadership habit this is.

As leaders, may we be the first ones to recognize and communicate how valuable the people we serve and work with are. As we celebrate our team, may we do so with excellence and by pointing others back to the greater vision we're all moving toward. May we be the first ones to encourage and affirm when team members work and lead with excellence.

And may we always pause to recognize the kind and guiding hand of the God who is active. May we be intentional to give Him the best of our celebration.

## Reflection & Discussion Questions

1. What are possible reasons why celebration can be an often-forgotten habit of leadership?

2. Why is celebrating the group or team we lead so important? What does it communicate?

3. What is an example of a time when you were affirmed or encouraged by a leader because of something you did with excellence? How did that affirmation make you feel?

## Coaching Moment

1. Ask your coach to share an example of something he or she has done (or has seen done) that celebrated a team or a group well.

2. What is one thing you could do to celebrate your team well? How would you do that and why do you think it would celebrate team members well? Who might be able to help you if you aren't great at fun? Share that idea with your coach and be open to his or her feedback.

# CONCLUSION

**W**ay back at the start, I shared that my goal was to *prime* you with biblical principles, practical habits, and effective strategies that would help you be a better leader, sooner. My prayer was that God would use *Primed To Lead* to add a little clay, width, depth, artistry, and solidity to your leadership. As I conclude this book, I want to share four favors I'd like to ask of you.

**First – Don't let the clay harden completely.**

As God continues to shape, mold, and solidify you as a leader, don't ever arrive at the place where you have no more pliability. While we remain on this side, where the Kingdom is not yet fully realized, you and I will not somehow *arrive* as perfect leaders. It is one thing to be *primed to lead*, but may we never fall into the trap of feeling as though we are too solid to still be shaped.

**Second – Prioritize practice.**

Practice the tools and habits provided in this book. Knowing the material does not mean we have mastered the practice. I can tell you, as the author of this book, in no way have I mastered these practices. Those who are excellent in a craft know they must continue to work at it. May we be excellent as we prioritize practice.

**Third – Pay it forward.**

Whatever help or encouragement this book has given you, I ask that you not keep it to yourself. As you continue to learn, grow, and be coached in leadership I ask that you would take steps to help other leaders to learn, grow, and even receive coaching from you! The baton of knowledge and wisdom should never stay with one runner, rather it should always be passed on. If this book has helped or encouraged you in any way, I humbly ask that you give a copy of *Primed To Lead* to the next person you believe it could help or encourage—and consider coaching the individual as he or she reads through it.

**Fourth – Stay secured to the One reliable anchor.**

In many ways, leadership really is like a climb. There are a lot of steps needed in order to move where we hope to go and where we hope to bring others along with us. My prayer for you is that the foundation of your leadership is completely tethered to who you are in Jesus Christ. As it is, may you lead with the end in mind…

As your legacy is shaped by God's activity,

For His glory,

And for the sake of His Kingdom being extended.

# ACKNOWLEDGEMENTS

*P*rimed *To Lead* does not exist without the wonderful people whose support and contributions made it possible. So, let me begin by thanking my incredible, beautiful wife **Katie**. Thank you for your support, patience, and sacrifice throughout this process.

To my parents, **Mark and Denise Warszawski** – thank you for being the first ones to help me cultivate a heart for the Lord, for being part of His Kingdom work, and for servant leadership. Thank you to the best in-laws, **Mark and Mary Leigh Wildermuth**, for never failing to give your love, care, and support.

To **Dave and Betsey Griffing, Dale and Kathie Roskom, and Bob and Selena Scheid.** Thank you for your friendship, for your investment in me, and for believing in me. Thank you for believing in the vision for this book and helping it to become a reality.

Thank you to my teammates at Lifepoint Church. **Dean Fulks**, thank you for your leadership, and for supporting me and this project. **Troy Palermo**, thank you for being *my* coach and always providing me with wise counsel, as well as encouragement. **Kristy Low**, thanks for the time and voice you gave in helping to make some of the key content and language of this book so much better. Thank you to Steve Clifton, Chad Grigsby, Paul Priddy, Nathan Shireman, and Shane Tucker for your friendship, help, and contributions.

Including many of the folks already mentioned, thank you to **the Christian leaders who gave voice to this book**. These voices include, but are not limited to: Denny Abbuhl, Tom Balliet, Trent Dunlap, David Fletcher, Steve Garcia, Derek Hahn, Mary Krell, Jim Mitchell, Kevin Oakley, Dan Owolabi, Brittany Stacey, and Daniel Wallace. A special thanks to Sherry Surratt in helping make this book better, especially for coaches. Geoff Surratt – thank you for your coaching on the front end of this writing project. Thank you to *Barna Group* for the superb research that helped shape this book.

To the best editor, **Allison Myers**. Thanks not only for your excellent work, but also for the coaching and encouragement you gave through the writing process. Thank you to **Kary Oberbrunner** and Author Academy Elite for publishing *Primed To Lead*. Kary, thank you for always being so gracious, supportive, and charitable.

Thank you to all the people who have invested in and supported me, especially in my early days of stepping into leadership. It was your leadership in my life that laid the foundation for *Primed To Lead*. Lastly, but most importantly, thank you to my Lord, Jesus Christ – my unceasing fountain of grace, goodness, and faithfulness.

# NOTES

**FOREWORD**
Rowe, Mike. September 29, 2018. "A Little Dab'll Do Ya." *The Way I Heard It.* MRW Holdings, LLC. September 29, 2018. Accessed April 20, 2020 https://mikerowe.com/2018/09/episode-69-a-little-dabll-do-ya/

**INTRODUCTION**
Maxwell, John C. *The 21 Irrefutable Laws of Leadership.* (Nashville, TN: Thomas Nelson, 2008.)

**CHAPTER 1: THE ANCHOR**
For more, please read chapter 5 of the book of Romans (in the Bible).
Johnson, Brian, Joel Case, Jonathan David Helser. 2015. *Jonathan David Helser, Melissa Helser: no longer slaves.* Redding, CA: Bethel Music.

## CHAPTER 2: COACHABLE

Goldman, David. "Disney to Buy Marvel for $4 Billion." CNNMoney. Cable News Network, August 31, 2009. https://money.cnn.com/2009/08/31/news/companies/disney_marvel/.

Whitten, Sarah. "Disney Bought Marvel for $4 Billion in 2009, a Decade Later It's Made More than $18 Billion at the Global Box Office." CNBC. CNBC, July 22, 2019. https://www.cnbc.com/2019/07/21/disney-has-made-more-than-18-billion-from-marvel-films-since-2012.html.

Nolan, Christopher, Charles Roven, Emma Thomas, David S. Goyer, Jonathan Nolan, Christian Bale, Heath Ledger, et al. 2008. *The Dark Knight*. Burbank, CA: Warner Home Video.

"H8085 - Shama` - Strong's Hebrew Lexicon (KJV)." Blue Letter Bible. Accessed April 12, 2020. https://www.blueletterbible.org/lang/lexicon/lexicon.cfm?t=kjv&strongs=h8085.

## CHAPTER 3: HAVE THE END IN MIND

Dickens, Charles H. *A Christmas Carol*. (London, England: Chapman & Hall, 1843.)

"Training Camp with the Cleveland Browns 01." *Hard Knocks*

## CHAPTER 4: TIME TO BE SHERLOCK

Covey, Stephen R. *The 7 Habits of Highly Effective People*. (San Francisco, CA: FranklinCovey Co., 2016.)

## CHAPTER 5: WHO AM I?

"Character." Merriam-Webster. Merriam-Webster. Accessed April 12, 2020. https://www.merriam-webster.com/dictionary/character.

"I Have A Dream," National Archives and Records Administration. Accessed April 12, 2020. https://www.archives.gov/files/press/exhibits/dream-speech.pdf.

## CHAPTER 6: EXCELLENCE

Kizer, Darren, Christine Kreisher, and Steph Whitacre. *The Volunteer Project: Stop Recruiting, Start Retaining.* (Atlanta, GA: 181 Publishing, 2015.)

## CHAPTER 8: RUBBING SHOULDERS

For more from Dan Owolabi, visit www.owolabileadership.com

Charan, Ram, Stephen J. Drotter, and James L. Noel. *The Leadership Pipeline: How to Build the Leadership Powered Company.* (Chichester: John Wiley, 2011.)

Manninen, Sandra, Lauri Tuominen, Robin I. Dunbar, Tomi Karjalainen, Jussi Hirvonen, Eveliina Arponen, Riitta Hari, Iiro P. Jääskeläinen, Mikko Sams, and Lauri Nummenmaa. "Social Laughter Triggers Endogenous Opioid Release in Humans." Journal of Neuroscience. Society for Neuroscience, June 21, 2017. https://www.jneurosci.org/content/37/25/6125.

## CHAPTER 9: TAKE IT TO THE BANK

"Account Passbook, 1817-23: RBS Heritage Hub." Accessed April 12, 2020. https://www.rbs.com/heritage/rbs-history-in-100-objects/history-in-100-themes/doing-business-openly-and-fairly/account-passbook-1817-23.html.

Murray-West, Rosie. "'Back to the Future' Savings Passbook Trumps the Internet." The Telegraph. Telegraph Media Group, June 12, 2012. https://www.telegraph.co.uk/finance/personalfinance/savings/9326252/Back-to-the-future-savings-passbook-trumps-the-internet.html.

For a resource to help you explore the call to ministry, check out "Discerning Your Call to Ministry: How to Know For Sure and What to Do About It" by Jason K. Allen.

## CHAPTER 11: BE PREPARED

For a sample *meeting agenda*, visit the resources page at www. primedtolead.com

## CHAPTER 12: THE LEADER & THE TEAM

Keller, Timothy J. *The Freedom of Self-Forgetfulness: the Path to True Christian Joy*. (Farington, UK: 10Publishing, 2014.)

Taylor, Justin, and Justin Taylor. "1,981 Years Ago Today: Why We Believe We Can Know the Exact Date Jesus Died." The Gospel Coalition, April 3, 2014. https://www.thegospelcoalition.org/blogs/justin-taylo r/1981-years-ago-today-why-we-believe-we-can-know-the-exact-date-jesus-died/.

Graham, Wyatt. "The First Twenty Years: What Happened to the Church Immediately after Jesus Died? - The Gospel Coalition: Canada." The Gospel Coalition | Canada, August 29, 2018. https://ca.thegospelcoalition.org/col umns/detrinitate/the-first-twenty-years-what-happene d-to-the-church-immediately-after-jesus-died/.

Stark, Rodney. *The Rise of Christianity: How the Obscure, Marginal Jesus Movement Became the Dominant Religious Force in the Western World in a Few Centuries*. (New York: HarperOne, 1997.)

Hackett, Conrad, and David McClendon. "World's Largest Religion by Population Is Still Christianity." Pew Research Center. Pew Research Center, April 5, 2017. https://www.pewresearch.org/fact-tank/2017/04/05/ christians-remain-worlds-largest-religious-grou p-but-they-are-declining-in-europe/.

## CHAPTER 13: THE STEWARD

Tolkien, J. R. R. *The Lord of the Rings*. (London: Harper Collins Publishers, 2014.)

www.yourenneagramcoach.com

Rath, Tom. *StrengthsFinder 2.0*. (New York, NY: Gallup Press, 2017.)

Visit www.primedtolead.com and visit the resources page to utilize a *spiritual gifts assessment* tool provided there. You can also search www.lifeway.com for their spiritual gifts assessment tools.

For help creating job descriptions, as well as other helpful resources for churches, visit www.xpastor.org

## CHAPTER 14: CULTURE CREATOR
Gold, Todd. 1989. *Michael Jackson: the man in the mirror*. London: Sidgwick & Jackson.

"Money." *The Office*

To learn more about Gull Lake Ministries Conference Center and Family Resort, visit www.gulllake.org

## CHAPTER 15: KNOW YOUR TARGET
Tisch, Steve, Wendy Finerman, Robert Zemeckis, Eric Roth, Tom Hanks, Robin Wright, Gary Sinise, Mykelti Williamson, Sally Field, and Winston Groom. 1995. *Forrest Gump*. [Hollywood, Calif.]: Paramount. https://archive.org/details/forrestgump0000unse.

For more from Geoff & Sherry Surratt, visit www.ministry-together.com

## CHAPTER 17: LEADING TEAMS WELL
"HR & Millennials: Insights Into Your New Human Capital." harp.ca. Human Resources Professionals Association, November 22, 2016. https://www.hrpa.ca/Documents/Public/Thought-Leadership/HRPA-Millennials-Report-20161122.pdf

Mehrabian, Albert. *Silent Messages: Implicit Communication of Emotions and Attitudes*. Belmont, CA: Wadsworth Pub. Co., 1981.

"Jeff Erlanger." Mister Rogers' Neighborhood. Accessed April 12, 2020. https://www.misterrogers.org/articles/jeffrey-erlanger/.

Rogers, Fred. 1970. *Fred Rogers: it's you I like.* Brentwood, TN: ClearBox Rights, LLC.

"Collaboration: Definition in the Cambridge English Dictionary." Collaboration | definition in the Cambridge English Dictionary. Accessed April 12, 2020. https://dictionary.cambridge.org/us/dictionary/english/collaboration.

**Chapter 18: TAKE TIME TO CELEBRATE**
"Launch Party." *The Office*

# ABOUT THE AUTHOR

## Chris Warszawski, M.A.

Serving in church leadership roles for over a decade, Chris' passion is to encourage leaders and families toward generational impact. He currently serves as the Family Ministries Pastor at Lifepoint Church in north Columbus, OH. Outreach Magazine named Lifepoint as one of the 100 fastest growing churches in America, as well as one of the top 3 multi-generational multiplying churches in America.

Chris earned his B.A. in Bible and Theology/Youth Ministry from Malone University, and he holds an M.A. in Theological Studies from Trinity Evangelical Divinity School.

Chris and his wife, Katie, have two wonderful children, Ella and Jacob. In the spring and summer, Chris enjoys spending time outside with his family. He especially enjoys family trips to the zoo, fishing with his kids, and yes – he still enjoys mowing the lawn. If you don't get that reference, then you need to read the book! For Chris, fall and winter in Ohio are best served with a good cup of coffee and watching a game of football with friends.

# LOOKING FOR MORE?

## Visit *PrimedToLead.com*

### MORE FOR LEADERS

Find more resources from Chris online, including tools to help you better apply the principles and strategies in *Primed To Lead*

### FREE E-BOOK FOR FAMILES

Parents, access a free resource designed to encourage and equip you with intentional discipleship habits as you lead in the home

### CONNECT

If there is way Chris can serve your team, group, or church - contact him at *PrimedToLead.com*